A FOX
IN A
BEAR TRAP

A BOOK ON
HOW TO
ASK FOR HELP

ADAM MAY, MS

Dedication

To my mother, my father, my grandparents, and anyone else who ever believed in me when I needed it most. Thank you for helping me when I thought I could not be helped.

Table of Contents

Preface...7

Chapter 1: Understanding Your Trap – Identifying Your Challenges 13

Chapter 2: Confronting Anxiety and Depression.................................22

Chapter 3: Overcoming Avoidance and Developing Emotional Maturity...33

Chapter 4: Shifting from Blaming to Taking Responsibility...............52

Chapter 5: Facing Fear and Identifying Fallacies.................................67

Chapter 6: Trust vs. Mistrust – Building Healthy Relationships........80

Chapter 7: Overcoming Helplessness, Hopelessness, and Worthlessness 93

Chapter 8: Enhancing Self-Worth and Addressing Worthlessness.....110

Chapter 9: Understanding Maslow's Hierarchy and Personal Growth..129

Chapter 10: Developing Personality and Identity – Addressing Distorted Thinking and Suicidal Ideations 150

Conclusion: The Power of Asking for Help – My Journey to Healing to truly help others 176

PREFACE

I sat in the sterile, dimly lit room, the cold blue light of the overhead fluorescent bulb casting harsh shadows across my face in the back basement of my parents' home. My hands, clammy and trembling, hovered over the keyboard. The email window was open in front of me, the cursor blinking in the void, waiting for words that seemed impossible to find. I took a deep breath, my chest tight, as I finally began to type.

Dear Sgt. Walters,

I paused, my finger hovering over the keys. I have been trying to write this letter for over a week. The words wouldn't come. Not in the way they should, anyway.

It wasn't just the legal trouble—though that was bad enough. It wasn't even the looming court date or the DUI charge that made me feel like a failure. It was the shame of who I'd become that night—the person who had driven drunk, who had ignored an officer's lawful order, resulting in being tased, who had acted out of frustration, grief, and anger that had nothing to do with the situation at hand. That person felt like a stranger to me now, but there had been a time when I believed that the worst thing I could ever do was let someone down.

And yet, here I was.

My name is Adam May, and I interacted with you in the early morning of the 15th and 16th at the Lee's Summit Police Station.

The words were a lifeline, pulling me back to that night. The flashing lights. The acrid smell of alcohol on my breath. Maybe a 5th deep by this point. The sirens were still ringing in my ears as I'd been led into the station. How had it all gone so wrong?

I had always prided myself on my professionalism. I was the guy who could take responsibility for his actions, who made the right choices—most of the time, anyway. But that night, everything had unraveled. The grief of losing my close friend, the post-traumatic stress of a cancer diagnosis, and the bitter mix of emotions I could no longer control—had all collided in a perfect storm. But none of it justified what had happened. None of it excused the reckless way I had behaved, the disrespect I had shown.

I continued typing, trying to make it right, trying to explain the unexplainable.

First and foremost, I want to directly apologize for my behavior prior to arriving at the station and during my initial intake. I am embarrassed for my actions and sincerely would like to apologize for any disrespect I may have shown towards you or any other officer.

The words tasted bitter and shameful as they left my fingertips, but they were true. I was embarrassed—hell, I was disgusted with myself. It was a feeling that gnawed at me every day. Every time I passed a police car, every time I heard a siren in the distance, the shame flooded me anew. Was that Officer there that night? Does that Officer know who I am?

I kept typing, unable to stop now.

I have been struggling with grief and loss recently, as well as some personal health issues that have come to light as well, but that is no excuse for my actions on that evening and my behavior.

The grief was still fresh. It wasn't something I could just turn off. And the health issues—well, they hadn't been the cause of my meltdown that night, but they were a part of the storm brewing inside me as the 10th anniversary of my diagnosis had just passed. My doctor had warned me that stress could manifest in strange ways. But no one had warned me it would make me into the kind of person who would take my anger out on the one thing that was supposed to protect me. I was ashamed of how it all played out.

But it was too late to have regrets now. All I could do was apologize, take accountability, and try to move forward.

I would like you to understand that the person that you and your fellow officers had to deal with that evening is by no means the person I am.

I wanted them to know that. I wanted the world to understand that this incident, this mistake, wasn't who I truly was. I wasn't some reckless fool, some man who thought the rules didn't apply to me. But in that moment, I had been all those things. I had been someone I barely recognized.

My fingers hovered over the keys once again, but the next words came more easily.

I have no excuse for my behavior, and again, I am extremely embarrassed.

I meant that. There were no excuses left, just the quiet certainty that things had to change. The problem wasn't just the alcohol or the mistakes of that night. It was the bigger issue I'd been running from—grief, fear, loneliness—that had spiraled me into that chaos.

As I hit "send," I sat back in my chair, the weight of the moment settled in. The letter wouldn't change what had happened, but it was a start to finally acknowledging that I needed help. This email became the first step, at least, toward taking responsibility and learning to ask for help.

This is the first step in becoming the person I know that I am capable of being—someone here to help others learn to ask for help before it is too late.

The Trap

To feel like a fox caught in a bear trap is to experience a profound, helpless kind of panic—a sharp, immediate pain that sears through your body and mind. It's the sudden realization that the freedom you once had is now reduced to a cold, unyielding confinement. Every attempt to escape only drives the trap deeper, intensifying the hurt. The world outside seems so close, so tangible, yet completely out of reach. And as the minutes stretch into hours, the weight of isolation presses harder. There's an acute awareness of your vulnerability, a quiet, gnawing desperation that claws at your spirit. You are caught between instinct and intellect, between fight and flight, and you can do nothing but wait for release that may never come.

Welcome to "A Fox in a Bear Trap," a workbook designed to help you navigate the complexities of asking for help while dealing with various emotional and psychological challenges. This workbook aims to guide you through understanding and overcoming obstacles such as anxiety, depression, avoidance, and distorted thinking. Through self-reflection, exercises, and practical strategies, you will build the skills needed to seek and accept help effectively.

Chapter 1:

Understanding Your Trap – Identifying Your Challenges

It starts quietly, like a shadow creeping at the edge of your vision. At first, you barely notice it, and then one day, you realize it has taken root, winding itself into every thought and every breath. You're trapped, but the walls are invisible. The cage isn't made of steel or wood but of your own mind—your own fears, your own wounds. The isolation sets in first. The world becomes a blur, everyone else moving in and out of their lives while you stand at the edges, watching through a fogged window, disconnected. The harder you reach to touch them, the more distant they become. You can't explain it, not even to yourself. It's as if you've become a stranger in your own skin.

And then there's the weight of the bottle, its steady comfort, the liquid warmth that dulls the edge of the pain. At first, it's just a way to cope, a momentary escape from the constant hum of anxiety, the intrusive thoughts that flood your mind when you least expect it. But soon, it becomes a pattern—a cycle that keeps you tethered to a false sense of relief, even as it drags you further into the darkness. Every drink or drug, every swallow or inhale, is a temporary silence, a pause from the raging storm inside your head. But when the bottle or bag is empty, the storm comes back fiercer than before, and you're left standing in the ruins of your own choices.

Then there's the weight of the past—the memories you've tried to bury, the images that return to haunt you when you're least prepared. Post-traumatic stress is a cruel ghost, one that doesn't just stay with you but constantly replays the worst moments, the moments where you felt powerless, broken, or afraid. And no matter how far you run, it follows you—silent, relentless. The anxiety tightens its grip around your chest, every door you try to open leading to another dead end, another reason to stay hidden in the dark. It's hard to breathe. It's hard to think clearly. It's even harder to admit that it's happening. That you're caught.

And then there's the deep well of depression, a sinking heaviness that swallows up the light. It's not just sadness but a numbness—a hollow ache that fills the spaces where hope once lived. Some days, it feels like you're underwater, trying to scream but unable to make a sound, struggling to move but unable to break the surface. You wonder if anyone can see you—if they even know you're still there, or if you've already disappeared.

This is your trap. Not one you chose, but one that formed around you, built from the very things that were meant to protect you—your coping mechanisms, your defense mechanisms, your ways of surviving the storm. But now, those same tools have become the bars of the cage. You're not just stuck in a moment; you're stuck in everything—a tangled mess of isolation, addiction, trauma, fear, and despair. The key to the trap is understanding what's holding you there. And the first step to escape is identifying the chains that bind you.

Objective:

Recognize and articulate the emotional and psychological barriers that are preventing you from asking for help.

Struggling with asking for help is a common experience and can stem from various psychological, emotional, and social factors. Here are some key reasons why people might find it difficult to ask for help:

- **Fear of Judgment or Rejection:** People often worry that asking for help will make them appear weak or inadequate, leading to fear of judgment or rejection from others.

- **Perceived Lack of Self-Reliance:** Some individuals equate asking for help with being dependent or incapable, and they may struggle with accepting that needing assistance does not diminish their self-worth.

- **Previous Negative Experiences:** Past experiences where seeking help led to negative outcomes, such as betrayal or invalidation, can make people hesitant to ask for support again.

- **Cultural and Societal Norms:** Cultural or societal expectations that value independence and self-sufficiency can discourage individuals from seeking help, as they may fear not meeting these norms.

- **Fear of Burdening Others:** There may be a concern about being a burden to others, making people reluctant to ask for help due to a fear of imposing or inconveniencing someone else.

- **Low Self-Esteem and Worthlessness:** Individuals with low self-esteem or feelings of worthlessness may feel unworthy of help or believe that their problems are not significant enough to warrant assistance.

- **Avoidance and Denial:** Avoidance behaviors and denial of the need for help can prevent individuals from seeking support. They might hope the problem will resolve on its own or be in denial about the severity of their situation.

- **Anxiety and Depression:** Anxiety and depression can create overwhelming feelings of helplessness and hopelessness, making the process of asking for help seem daunting or insurmountable.

- **Lack of Awareness:** Some individuals may not fully recognize their need for help or may have difficulty articulating their needs, making it hard to reach out effectively.

- **Distorted Thinking Patterns:** Cognitive distortions, such as catastrophizing or all-or-nothing thinking, can lead to unrealistic expectations about how asking for help will be received or its potential outcomes.

- **Personality Traits:**Personality traits, such as high levels of perfectionism or introversion, can impact one's comfort level while seeking help. Perfectionists may fear that asking for help reveals flaws, while introverts may find it more challenging to reach out.

- **Lack of Skills or Knowledge:**Some people might not know how to ask for help effectively or might not have the skills to communicate their needs clearly, leading to reluctance.

Exercises 1.1:

Reflective Journaling: Write about specific instances where you felt stuck or unable to seek help.

____

____

____

____

____

____

____

____

Exercise 1.2: Self-Assessment Quiz: Evaluate Your Current Emotional State & Identify Key Challenges

Instructions: For each statement below, rate how true it feels for you on a scale of 1 to 5, with 1 being "Strongly Disagree" and 5 being "Strongly Agree."

Emotional Awareness & State

1. I rarely feel overwhelmed by my emotions.

    1 ☐ 2 ☐ 3 ☐ 4 ☐ 5 ☐

2. I find it easy to identify what I'm feeling in the moment.

    1 ☐ 2 ☐ 3 ☐ 4 ☐ 5 ☐

3. I feel generally happy or content with my life right now.

    1 ☐ 2 ☐ 3 ☐ 4 ☐ 5 ☐

4. I express my emotions well instead of bottling them up.

    1 ☐ 2 ☐ 3 ☐ 4 ☐ 5 ☐

5. I don't often experience anxiety or worry about the future.

    1 ☐ 2 ☐ 3 ☐ 4 ☐ 5 ☐

Current Stressors & Challenges

1. I am currently facing no major life challenges (e.g., work, relationships, health).

    1 ☐ 2 ☐ 3 ☐ 4 ☐ 5 ☐

2. I feel like I manage my current responsibilities or commitments well.

1 ☐ 2 ☐ 3 ☐ 4 ☐ 5 ☐

3. I maintain balance between my work, personal life, and self-care.

1 ☐ 2 ☐ 3 ☐ 4 ☐ 5 ☐

4. I feel supported when dealing with personal challenges.

1 ☐ 2 ☐ 3 ☐ 4 ☐ 5 ☐

5. I often feel like I'm able to move forward with certain aspects of my life without feeling stuck.

1 ☐ 2 ☐ 3 ☐ 4 ☐ 5 ☐

Coping & Resilience

1. I am able to bounce back quickly from setbacks or disappointments.

1 ☐ 2 ☐ 3 ☐ 4 ☐ 5 ☐

2. I actively engage in activities or practices that help me manage stress (e.g., exercise, meditation, hobbies).

1 ☐ 2 ☐ 3 ☐ 4 ☐ 5 ☐

3. I find it easy to relax or disconnect from my stressors.

1 ☐ 2 ☐ 3 ☐ 4 ☐ 5 ☐

4. I feel hopeful about overcoming my current challenges.

1 ☐ 2 ☐ 3 ☐ 4 ☐ 5 ☐

Reflection

1. I regularly take time to reflect on my emotional well-being.

   1 ☐ 2 ☐ 3 ☐ 4 ☐ 5 ☐

2. I feel well connected to my own needs or desires.

   1 ☐ 2 ☐ 3 ☐ 4 ☐ 5 ☐

3. I tend to face difficult emotions or situations, without avoiding or hoping they will resolve on their own.

   1 ☐ 2 ☐ 3 ☐ 4 ☐ 5 ☐

Scoring and Reflection:

1-20: You may be feeling emotionally overwhelmed or disconnected. It's important to check in with your emotional needs and consider seeking support, whether through self-care, talking with loved ones, or professional help.

21-40: You may be experiencing some emotional strain but have some capacity to manage. Reflect on areas where you might benefit from additional support or coping strategies. It's okay to ask for help.

41-60: You are generally managing your emotions well but might still be facing some stressors or challenges. Continue practicing self-care and resilience-building strategies to maintain emotional balance.

61-85: You are feeling emotionally balanced and resilient. Keep practicing your current strategies, but also remain mindful of any shifts in your emotional state. Regular reflection can help you maintain your well-being.

Next Steps:

- **If you scored lower in emotional awareness,** consider journaling or speaking with a counselor to explore your emotions more deeply.

- **If you scored higher in stress or challenges,** reflect on where you may need additional support. This could be seeking help from a mentor or therapist or making time for relaxation.

- **If you feel stuck or overwhelmed,** take small steps to break down your challenges into manageable tasks and celebrate small wins along the way.

Confronting Anxiety and Depression

There are days when the weight of the world feels like a hundred-pound anchor chained to your chest, dragging you down with every breath. Anxiety and depression aren't just feelings—they're presence, heavy and suffocating. They settle in like unwanted guests who refuse to leave, making even the smallest task feel impossible. The constant hum of fear, the tightness in your chest, the unrelenting urge to escape your own thoughts. It's a restless, gnawing tension that never really lets up, yet it's never loud enough to scream for help. It's more like a shadow, ever-present and suffocating, clouding everything you try to do, every conversation, every moment. You can't quite explain it to others because how can you describe something that seems to live deep inside you, something that no one can see?

There's a part of you that longs for connection, but isolation feels safer, even though it only feeds the monsters inside your mind. The loneliness is thick, a kind of silence that wraps itself around your life like a suffocating fog. The people around you try to reach out, but you're just... not there. You can't meet their eyes or bring yourself to say the words you know they need to hear. So you push them away, retreating into the numb comfort of your own company. After all, it's easier to face the monsters inside when no one else is watching. Easier to bury the pain in a bottle, to let the alcohol drown out the noise of your thoughts, if only for a little while.

But the thing with alcohol and substance—and the things we use to numb ourselves—is that they don't silence the pain. They just make it harder to feel. They keep you in a holding pattern, stuck in a loop where each day is a repetition of the last, the same struggle to stay afloat in an ocean that keeps pulling you under. You drink or drug to forget, but in truth, all you're doing is building a wall between yourself and the world, between yourself and the reality of what's happening to you. And eventually, the drinking or using stops being a choice. It's just a way of surviving—just another symptom of the anxiety, depression, and trauma that you don't know how to face.

The past is never far behind. The memories you've tried to bury, the trauma that lingers like a dark cloud—you try to outrun it, but it's always there, just beneath the surface, whispering when you least expect it. Post-traumatic stress is a constant reminder of your vulnerability, a never-ending loop of fear and flashbacks that catch you off guard. It's like living in a house without doors, windows, or way out. And with every drink, every moment of isolation, you think you're running from it, but you're not. You're just giving it more power.

But here's the thing: you can't outrun your mind forever. The longer you deny it, the harder it becomes to breathe. The harder it becomes to live. And eventually, you realize that the only way out isn't through avoidance or numbness but through facing the very things you've spent years running from—anxiety, depression, trauma. You have to confront them, not as enemies, but as parts of yourself that need to be heard. You have to name them, face them, and sit with them long enough to understand that they don't define you. It's a terrifying idea. It means letting go of the only defenses you've ever known. But it's the first step toward breaking the cycle. The first step toward reclaiming your life.

What is first required is an understanding of what you are facing.

Objective: Learn strategies to manage anxiety and depression that may hinder your ability to ask for help.

Emotional and Psychological Symptoms of Depression:

1. **Persistent Sadness:** Feeling overwhelmingly sad or empty most of the day, nearly every day.

2. **Loss of Interest or Pleasure:** Losing interest in activities or hobbies that once brought joy or satisfaction.

3. **Feelings of Hopelessness or Helplessness:** A pervasive sense of despair or a belief that things will never improve.

4. **Low Self-Esteem:** Experiencing feelings of worthlessness or guilt, often accompanied by self-criticism.

5. **Difficulty Concentrating:** Trouble focusing, making decisions, or remembering things.

6. **Irritability:** Becoming unusually irritable or easily frustrated over minor issues.

Physical Symptoms:

1. **Changes in Appetite or Weight:** Significant weight loss or gain due to changes in eating habits.

2. **Sleep Disturbances:** Experiencing insomnia (difficulty sleeping) or hypersomnia (excessive sleeping).

3. **Fatigue or Loss of Energy:** Feeling constantly tired or lacking the energy to complete daily tasks.

4. **Physical Aches and Pains:** Unexplained physical symptoms such as headaches, back pain, or stomachaches.

Behavioral Symptoms:

1. **Withdrawal from Social Activities:** Isolating oneself from friends, family, and social activities.

2. **Neglecting Responsibilities:** Difficulty managing daily responsibilities, such as work, school, or home duties.

3. **Changes in Activity Level:** Either a significant decrease in activity or restlessness and agitation.

Cognitive Symptoms:

1. **Negative Thought Patterns:** Persistent negative thinking, including self-blame and thoughts of inadequacy.

2. **Difficulty Making Decisions:** Struggling to make decisions or feeling indecisive.

3. **Distorted Perception of Reality:** Viewing situations in a more negative light or having a skewed perception of oneself and the world.

Severe Symptoms:

1. **Thoughts of Death or Suicide:** Experiencing thoughts about dying or contemplating suicide.

2. **Inability to Function:** Difficulty performing everyday tasks to the extent that it severely impacts one's quality of life.

How It Feels:

1. **Overwhelming Despair:** A pervasive feeling of sadness or emptiness that feels all-encompassing and difficult to escape.

2. **Emotional Numbness:** A sense of emotional numbness or detachment from one's feelings or surroundings.

3. **Exhaustion:** Feeling emotionally and physically drained, even without significant exertion.

4. **Isolation:** A profound sense of loneliness despite being around others and a desire to withdraw from social interactions.

Individual Variations:

It's important to note that depression can look and feel different for each person. Some might experience more physical symptoms, while others may struggle primarily with emotional or cognitive issues. The severity and combination of symptoms can also vary widely.

If you or someone you know is experiencing symptoms of depression, seeking help from a mental health professional is crucial. Depression is a treatable condition, and professional support can provide effective strategies for managing and overcoming the symptoms.

Emotional and Psychological Symptoms of Anxiety:

1. **Excessive Worry:** Persistent and uncontrollable worry about everyday situations or potential future events, often with a sense of impending doom.
2. **Restlessness:** Feeling on edge, unable to relax, or experiencing a constant sense of unease.
3. **Difficulty Concentrating:** Struggling to focus on tasks or find that your mind frequently drifts to anxious thoughts.
4. **Irritability:** Being easily annoyed or experiencing heightened frustration over minor issues.
5. **Fear of Loss of Control:** A strong fear of losing control over one's mind or body or fear of a panic attack.

Physical Symptoms:

1. **Increased Heart Rate:** A rapid or pounding heartbeat, often felt in the chest or neck.

2. **Sweating:** Excessive sweating, even in the absence of physical exertion or heat.

3. **Shaking or Trembling:** Noticeable trembling or shaking, often in the hands or legs.

4. **Muscle Tension:** Persistent muscle tightness, especially in the shoulders, neck, and jaw.

5. **Shortness of Breath:** Feeling as though you can't catch your breath or experiencing a sensation of tightness in the chest.

6. **Dizziness or Lightheadedness:** A sensation of dizziness, feeling faint, or lightheadedness.

7. **Nausea:** Experiencing gastrointestinal discomfort, nausea, or a churning stomach.

8. **Fatigue:** Feeling unusually tired or drained despite adequate rest.

Behavioral Symptoms:

1. **Avoidance:** Avoiding situations or places that trigger anxiety, which can lead to social isolation or difficulties in daily functioning.

2. **Compulsive Behaviors:** Engaging in repetitive or ritualistic behaviors to alleviate anxiety, such as excessive checking or cleaning.

3. **Restlessness:** Physical restlessness, such as fidgeting, pacing, or difficulty sitting still.

Cognitive Symptoms:

1. **Racing Thoughts:** Experiencing a rapid stream of thoughts, often focusing on worst-case scenarios or irrational fears.

2. **Catastrophizing:** Expecting the worst possible outcome in situations, leading to heightened fear and distress.

3. **Overthinking:** Getting caught up in a cycle of over-analyzing and worrying about potential problems or decisions.

How It Feels:

1. **Overwhelming Unease:** A persistent and overwhelming sense of discomfort or dread, even when there is no immediate threat.

2. **Hypervigilance:** Being excessively alert or watchful for potential dangers or threats, leading to heightened sensitivity to one's environment.

3. **Disconnection:** Feeling disconnected from reality or oneself, sometimes described as a sense of detachment or unreality.

4. **Impaired Functioning:** Difficulty performing daily tasks or engaging in activities due to the impact of anxiety on your focus and energy levels.

Anxiety can vary widely among individuals. Some may experience it primarily as physical symptoms, while others might feel it more intensely as emotional or cognitive disturbances. The severity and specific symptoms can differ based on the type of anxiety disorder (e.g., generalized anxiety disorder, panic disorder, social anxiety disorder).

If you or someone you know is struggling with anxiety, seeking support from a mental health professional can provide effective strategies for managing and reducing symptoms. Therapy, medication, and lifestyle changes can all play a role in alleviating anxiety and improving overall well-being.

Exercise 2.1:Cognitive Behavioral Techniques: Identify and challenge negative thoughts.

Objective: This exercise will help you become more aware of negative thoughts, assess their accuracy, and reframe them with a more balanced perspective.

Step 1: Identify a Negative Thought

Think of a recent situation where you felt upset, anxious, or discouraged. Write down the negative thoughts that came to your mind at that moment.

Example Negative Thought:

"I'm not good enough to succeed."

Your Negative Thought:

____

____

Step 2: Challenge the Thought

Now, examine your thoughts. Ask yourself the following questions to challenge its accuracy:

1. Is this thought based on facts or assumptions?
2. What evidence do I have that supports this thought?
3. What evidence contradicts this thought?
4. Am I overgeneralizing or making this seem worse than it really is?

Example Challenge:

*   Evidence for: "I've failed a few times before."
*   Evidence against: "I've also succeeded in similar situations, and I've learned from past mistakes."

Your Evidence for and Against:

*   Evidence for: _______________________________________
*   Evidence against: ___________________________________

Step 3: Reframe the Thought

Take a moment to reframe your negative thoughts in a more balanced, realistic way. It doesn't need to be overly positive, just more grounded in reality.

Example Reframe:

"I've had setbacks, but I've also had successes. I can learn from this and try again."

Your Reframed Thought:

____

____

Step 4: Reflect on How You Feel

After reframing the thought, check in with yourself (Rate from 1 to 10):

- How did the negative thought make you feel before?
  1 ☐ 2 ☐ 3 ☐ 4 ☐ 5 ☐ 6 ☐ 7 ☐ 8 ☐ 9 ☐ 10 ☐
- How do you feel now after reframing it? (Rate from 1 to 10)
  1 ☐ 2 ☐ 3 ☐ 4 ☐ 5 ☐ 6 ☐ 7 ☐ 8 ☐ 9 ☐ 10 ☐

Reflection:

This exercise is a way to recognize negative patterns in your thinking and challenge them to create a more realistic, balanced view of the situation. The more you practice this, the easier it becomes to shift negative thoughts and respond more positively.

Exercise 2.2: Mindfulness Practice: Engage in exercises to reduce anxiety and improve emotional regulation.

Overcoming Avoidance and Developing Emotional Maturity

Avoidance is the quiet killer of potential. It's the impulse to turn away from discomfort, to sweep emotions under the rug, and to pretend that if you ignore the hard stuff long enough, it will disappear. But avoidance doesn't make things go away; it only allows them to grow, fester, and poison everything you care about—your life, relationships, success, and sense of self-worth.

When you avoid life's challenges, you avoid growth. You stay stuck in patterns that limit your potential, clinging to the safety of what's familiar rather than venturing into the unknown, where true growth happens. This stagnation is especially damaging in relationships and families. When you avoid difficult conversations, withhold vulnerability, or refuse to face the emotional messes that inevitably arise, you erode trust. The walls between you and the people you love grow higher, the distance becomes more palpable, and the connection you once had begins to fray at the edges. Avoidance fosters isolation, and without the emotional maturity to confront those hard moments, the gap between you and those who matter most continues to widen, often beyond repair.

The same is true when it comes to success. Avoidance is the enemy of ambition. It convinces you that failure is something to fear, that striving toward your goals is too hard, too risky. So, instead of pushing forward, you retreat into a comfort zone that feels safer in the short term but leaves you unfulfilled and unaccomplished. Without the emotional maturity to face setbacks with resilience and without learning to push through discomfort, you never unlock your true potential. You hold yourself back, unsure of your own strength, too afraid to fail or to risk the possibility of falling short.

Perhaps the most insidious damage caused by avoidance is the inability to ask for help. Emotional maturity is not about being able to handle everything on your own; it's about recognizing your limitations, acknowledging your needs, and reaching out when you need support. But when you're trapped in avoidance, asking for help feels like a weakness. You become convinced that you should be able to do it alone and that asking for help is an admission of failure. But in truth, asking for help is one of the most courageous, mature things you can do—it's an acknowledgment that you are human and that your strength comes not from going it alone but from knowing when to lean on others.

Avoidance keeps you trapped in a cycle of self-reliance gone too far, but emotional maturity allows you to break free. It teaches you to embrace discomfort, face the hard things head-on, and reach out for help when needed. Only then can you move forward—not just in your goals but in your relationships, your success, and your growth as a person. Only then can you begin to live fully, honestly, and without the burden of avoiding what you fear. We all have ways of coping with discomfort—whether it's turning away from difficult emotions, procrastinating on tasks we fear, or shutting down in the face of conflict. But avoidance, while it may offer temporary relief, only deepens the very anxiety and depression we hope to escape. In this chapter, we'll explore how to break the cycle of avoidance that keeps us stuck and how developing emotional maturity can open the door to healthier ways of managing our feelings and relationships.

Emotional maturity isn't about suppressing or ignoring our emotions; it's about learning to feel them fully, respond to them wisely, and face the challenges they bring with courage and clarity. It's about taking responsibility for our emotional landscape so that asking for help—whether from a friend, a therapist, or a loved one—becomes not an overwhelming burden but a natural part of our healing process.

By examining the roots of avoidance—whether it's the fear of judgment, the pressure of perfectionism, or the inner dialogue of unworthiness—we'll uncover practical tools for building resilience. We'll explore how embracing vulnerability can be a powerful antidote to anxiety and how moving through discomfort can ultimately lead to greater peace and emotional balance.

In this chapter, you'll learn how to recognize the patterns of avoidance in your own life, understand their impact on your mental health, and develop the emotional maturity to face them head-on. Most importantly, you'll discover how to begin asking for help with less fear and more confidence, as well as the understanding that seeking support is not a sign of weakness but a testament to your strength and commitment to growth.

Objective: Address avoidance behaviors and work towards greater emotional maturity.

Overcoming avoidance involves addressing the underlying fears and anxieties that drive it and developing practical strategies to face and manage the situations you're avoiding. Here's a structured approach to help you overcome avoidance:

1. Identify the Avoidance:

- **Recognize What You're Avoiding:** Identify specific situations, tasks, or people that you tend to avoid. Journaling or making a list can help clarify what you're avoiding and why.

- **Understand the Triggers:** Reflect on what triggers your avoidance. Are there specific thoughts, feelings, or situations that prompt you to avoid?

2. Understand the Underlying Causes:

- **Explore Your Fears:** Understand the fears or anxieties driving your avoidance. Are you afraid of failure, criticism, or the unknown?

- **Assess Your Beliefs:** Examine any underlying beliefs or assumptions that contribute to your avoidance. For example, do you believe you're not capable of handling certain tasks?

3. Challenge Negative Thoughts:

- **Identify Cognitive Distortions:** Recognize any negative or distorted thinking patterns, such as catastrophizing or all-or-nothing thinking, that contribute to your avoidance.

- **Reframe Your Thoughts:** Practice challenging and reframing these negative thoughts with more balanced and realistic perspectives.

4. Gradual Exposure:

- **Start Small:** Begin by facing less intimidating aspects of the situations you're avoiding. Break down tasks into smaller, more manageable steps.

- **Increase Gradually:** Gradually increase the difficulty or intensity of the situations you're facing as you become more comfortable and confident.

5. Set Achievable Goals:

- **Create Specific Goals:** Set clear, achievable goals for addressing your avoidance. For example, if you're avoiding social events, set a goal to attend a small gathering.

- **Track Progress:** Monitor your progress and celebrate small victories along the way. This helps build confidence and motivation.

6. Develop Coping Strategies:

- **Use Relaxation Techniques:** Practice relaxation techniques, such as deep breathing, mindfulness, or progressive muscle relaxation, to manage anxiety associated with avoidance.

- **Practice Self-Care:** Engage in activities that promote well-being and reduce stress, such as exercise, hobbies, or spending time with supportive people.

7. Seek Support:

- **Talk to a Therapist:** Cognitive-behavioral therapy (CBT) can be particularly effective for addressing avoidance behaviors. A therapist can help you identify avoidance patterns and develop coping strategies.

- **Join Support Groups:** Support groups can provide encouragement and advice from others who have faced similar challenges.

8. Develop Problem-Solving Skills:

- **Identify Solutions:** Work on developing problem-solving skills to address the issues causing you to avoid certain situations. This might involve brainstorming solutions and evaluating their feasibility.

- **Practice Decision-Making:** Improve your decision-making skills to reduce indecision and the anxiety associated with it.

9. Build Self-Efficacy:

- **Focus on Strengths:** Identify and leverage your strengths and past successes to build confidence in your ability to handle challenging situations.

- **Develop Resilience:** Work on building resilience by learning from setbacks and continuing to try, even when faced with difficulties.

10. Reevaluate Your Goals:

- **Assess Your Priorities:** Reflect on your goals and priorities to ensure they align with your values and long-term aspirations. Sometimes, avoidance is a sign that a goal or task needs to be reevaluated.

- **Adjust Your Approach:** Be flexible and willing to adjust your approach if necessary. It's okay to modify your goals or strategies as you learn more about what works for you.

Developing emotional maturity involves cultivating self-awareness, self-regulation, empathy, and effective communication skills. It's a process of growing in understanding and managing your emotions while navigating relationships with others in a healthy, balanced way.

Here's a step-by-step guide to help you develop emotional maturity:

1. Cultivate Self-Awareness:

- **Reflect on Your Emotions:** Regularly take time to reflect on how you're feeling and why. Journaling can help you explore your emotional responses and triggers.

- **Understand Your Triggers:** Identify situations, people, or events that trigger strong emotional reactions. Understanding these triggers can help you manage your responses more effectively.

- **Seek Feedback:** Ask trusted friends, family members, or colleagues for honest feedback about how you handle emotions and relationships. Use this feedback to gain insight into areas for growth.

2. Practice Self-Regulation:

- **Learn Emotional Regulation Techniques:** Develop strategies to manage and modulate your emotions, such as deep breathing, mindfulness, or progressive muscle relaxation.

- **Develop Coping Skills:** Use coping mechanisms like problem-solving, rethinking perspectives, or engaging in physical activities to handle stress and emotional upheaval.

- **Pause and Reflect:** Before reacting to strong emotions, take a pause to reflect. This can prevent impulsive decisions and help you respond more thoughtfully.

3. Enhance Empathy:

- **Listen Actively:** Practice active listening by focusing fully on the speaker, acknowledging their feelings, and avoiding interruptions.

- **Put Yourself in Others' Shoes:** Try to understand situations from other people's perspectives. This helps build empathy and fosters better interpersonal relationships.

- **Express Understanding:** Show empathy through your responses. Use phrases like "I understand how you feel" or "That must be really difficult for you."

4. Improve Communication Skills:

- **Practice Assertiveness:** Communicate your needs and feelings clearly and respectfully without being aggressive or passive. Assertiveness helps you express yourself while respecting others.

- **Handle Conflicts Constructively:** Approach conflicts with a problem-solving attitude. Focus on finding solutions rather than placing blame.

- **Use "I" Statements:** When discussing feelings, use "I" statements (e.g., "I feel upset when..."). This helps in expressing your emotions without accusing or blaming others.

5. Develop Resilience:

- **Adapt to Change:** Embrace change and uncertainty with flexibility. Developing resilience helps you manage setbacks and adapt to new situations effectively.

- **Learn from Challenges:** View challenges as opportunities for growth. Reflect on what you've learned from difficult experiences and how you can apply these lessons.

6. Foster Self-Compassion:

- **Be Kind to Yourself:** Practice self-compassion by treating yourself with kindness and understanding, especially during times of failure or difficulty.

- **Avoid Self-Criticism:** Challenge negative self-talk and focus on your strengths and achievements. Recognize that everyone makes mistakes and that these are opportunities for learning.

7. Build Healthy Relationships:

- **Set Boundaries:** Establish and maintain healthy boundaries in relationships to protect your emotional well-being and respect others' boundaries.

- **Seek and Offer Support:** Build a support network of friends, family, or mentors who can provide encouragement and advice. Be willing to offer support to others as well.

8. Embrace Personal Growth:

- **Pursue Personal Development:** Engage in activities or practices that foster personal growth, such as reading self-help books, attending workshops, or participating in therapy.

- **Set Goals for Growth:** Identify areas where you want to improve and set specific, achievable goals. Track your progress and celebrate milestones along the way.

9. Practice Mindfulness and Reflection:

- **Engage in Mindfulness:** Practice mindfulness to stay present and aware of your emotions and thoughts. Techniques like meditation can enhance self-awareness and emotional regulation.

- **Reflect on Experiences:** Regularly reflect on your interactions, decisions, and emotional responses. Use this reflection to identify patterns and areas for improvement.

10. Seek Professional Help if Needed:

- **Consider Therapy:** Working with a therapist can provide valuable insights and tools for developing emotional maturity. Therapy can help you address underlying issues and build healthier emotional habits.

- **Join Support Groups:** Support groups can offer a sense of community and shared experiences, providing additional perspectives and encouragement.

Exercises 3: Avoidance Patterns: Map out situations where you tend to avoid seeking help.

Objective: To identify situations where you typically avoid seeking help, explore the reasons behind this avoidance, and reflect on healthier alternatives.

Exercise 3.1

Step 1: Identify Situations of Avoidance

Think about recent situations where you faced a challenge but chose not to ask for help. These could be work-related, personal, or emotional situations.

Example Situations:

- Not asking a colleague for assistance on a project.
- Avoiding telling a friend you're struggling with your mental health.
- Not reaching out for support when feeling overwhelmed at work.

Write down 2-3 situations where you avoided seeking help:

____

____

____

Step 2: Explore Your Reasons for Avoidance

For each situation you wrote down, reflect on why you didn't seek help. Did you fear judgment, feel like a burden, or believe you should handle it on your own?

Example Reasons for Avoidance:

- "I didn't want to appear weak or incompetent."
- "I felt like I should be able to manage it myself."
- "I didn't want to bother anyone."

Write down the reasons you avoided seeking help for each situation:

Step 3: Challenge Your Beliefs About Seeking Help

Now, examine the reasons you avoided seeking help. Are they based on facts, or do they reflect distorted thinking (e.g., fear of judgment, self-criticism)?

Example Challenge:

"I thought asking for help would make me look weak, but asking for help is actually a sign of strength and self-awareness."

Write a more balanced perspective for each reason you identified:

Step 4: Plan for Change

Now that you've reflected on the situations and reasons for avoiding help, think about how you can handle similar situations differently in the future. What small step can you take to be more open to seeking support?

Example Action Plan:

"Next time I'm struggling with a project, I will ask a colleague for help with one specific task."

Your Action Plan:

Step 5: Reflect on the Benefits of Seeking Help

Consider how seeking help could improve your situation. How might it make things easier, reduce stress, or help you grow?

Write down 1-2 potential benefits of seeking help:

Reflection:

This exercise can help you recognize where avoidance may be affecting your personal or professional growth. With increased awareness and small changes, you can gradually shift from avoiding help to feeling more comfortable seeking it when necessary.

Emotional Maturity Checklist: Assess and develop skills related to emotional maturity.

Objective: To assess your emotional maturity and identify areas to develop for better emotional regulation, communication, and personal growth.

Exercise 3.2

Self-Awareness

- I can identify my emotions as they arise (e.g., I know when I'm feeling angry, anxious, or happy).
- I regularly reflect on my emotional reactions to situations.
- I am able to recognize patterns in my emotions and behaviors.

Emotional Regulation

- I can manage strong emotions (like anger, sadness, or frustration) without letting them control my actions.
- I use healthy coping strategies (e.g., deep breathing, exercising, talking to a friend) when I feel overwhelmed.
- I am able to pause and think before reacting in emotionally charged situations.

Responsibility for Actions

- I take responsibility for my emotions, actions, and mistakes without blaming others.
- I can admit when I am wrong and am open to constructive feedback.
- I try to make amends when my actions negatively affect others.

Communication Skills

- I am able to express my emotions clearly and respectfully without bottling them up or being overly aggressive.
- I listen actively when others share their feelings or concerns without interrupting or judging.
- I am open to having difficult conversations and addressing conflicts directly.

Empathy & Compassion

- I try to understand the feelings of others, even if I don't agree with their perspective.

- I am considerate of how my words and actions affect other people.
- I show kindness and support to others, even when I'm stressed or busy.

Self-Control & Patience

- I am able to delay gratification when necessary (e.g., resisting impulsive decisions or emotional reactions).
- I remain patient and composed when facing delays, frustrations, or setbacks.
- I don't let temporary emotions cloud my long-term goals or values.

Resilience & Adaptability

- I can bounce back after facing a failure or disappointment, learning from the experience.
- I am flexible when things don't go as planned, adjusting my expectations and actions as needed.
- I maintain a hopeful outlook even during challenging times, trusting that things will improve.

Interpersonal Boundaries

- I respect other people's boundaries and expect the same in return.
- I am able to set healthy boundaries with others and communicate them clearly when needed.

- I can say "no" when I need to protect my time, energy, or well-being.

Personal Growth

- I actively seek personal growth, learning from mistakes and striving to improve.
- I'm open to new ideas and willing to change behaviors that are not serving me.
- I prioritize self-care and well-being to ensure I am emotionally equipped to handle life's challenges.

Reflection & Action Plan

- What area(s) do you want to focus on for personal growth?

____

____

- What is one specific action you can take this week to develop your emotional maturity?

____

____

Scoring:

- **Mostly "Yes" answers**: You are demonstrating a high level of emotional maturity. Keep nurturing these skills for continued growth.

- **Some "No" answers**: Emotional maturity is a skill that can always be developed. Focus on the areas where you see room for improvement.

- **Mostly "No" answers**: It's normal to have areas for growth. Start by picking one or two areas from the checklist to focus on, and gradually work toward developing those skills.

Shifting from Blaming to Taking Responsibility

There's a kind of comfort in blame. It's easy, quick, and offers a temporary sense of relief. When things go wrong, when life feels unfair or overwhelming, blaming someone or something outside yourself is an almost automatic response. It shifts the weight off your shoulders, even if only for a moment, and gives you the illusion of control. But here's the truth: blame doesn't change anything. It doesn't heal wounds, fix problems, or move you forward. It keeps you stuck—trapped in a cycle of resentment and powerlessness. The more you blame, the less you're able to see your own role in the story. And the less you see your own role, the less you can change it.

Shifting from blame to responsibility is one of the hardest but most necessary transformations you can make. It requires humility, courage, and the willingness to face uncomfortable truths about yourself and your life. When you take responsibility, you stop pointing fingers and start looking inward. You begin to ask the hard questions: What can I control? How did I contribute to this situation? What choices have led me here? This isn't about self-criticism or guilt; it's about empowerment. Because when you take responsibility, you take ownership of your life, choices, and actions. You stop being a passive observer and become an active participant in your own healing and growth.

But here's where the shift becomes particularly transformative: taking responsibility also means learning to ask for help. This is where most people get stuck. Taking responsibility often feels like you're supposed to do it all on your own as if asking for help is an admission that you've failed or are incapable. But that's the lie. Asking for help is not a sign of weakness; it's a sign of strength—and maturity. It means recognizing that you can't do it all by yourself and that it's okay to lean on others when you need support. In fact, it's often the first step toward true responsibility.

When you blame others, you give away your power. When you take responsibility, you reclaim it. And part of that reclamation is understanding that asking for help is part of the process. It's not about having all the answers—it's about being honest enough with yourself to know that you can't always carry the burden alone. The moment you stop blaming and start taking responsibility for your life, you'll find that you have more control than you ever realized.

You'll also find that asking for help isn't a weakness—it's a tool for growth, a step toward greater emotional maturity, and a key to unlocking the potential within you.

Objective: Move from a mindset of blaming others to one of personal accountability and growth.

Shifting from blaming to taking ownership is crucial in personal growth and effective problem-solving. It involves moving from a mindset of placing responsibility on external factors or others to acknowledging and accepting your role in situations and focusing on what you can control. Here's a structured approach to help you make this shift:

1. Acknowledge the Blame:

- Recognize When You're Blaming: Pay attention to moments when you're blaming others or external factors. Notice the language you use and the patterns of thinking.

- Reflect on the Impact: Consider how blaming others affects your relationships, problem-solving, and personal growth. Understanding the consequences can motivate you to shift your approach.

2. Examine Your Role:

- Identify Your Contributions: Reflect on your own actions, decisions, or behaviors that may have contributed to the situation. Ask yourself, "What role did I play in this outcome?"

- Assess Your Reactions: Consider how your reactions, communication style, or choices might have influenced the situation. Self-awareness is key to understanding your part in any issue.

3. Shift Your Perspective:

- Focus on Solutions: Instead of dwelling on who is at fault, shift your focus to finding solutions and making improvements. Ask yourself, "What can I do to address this issue?"

- Adopt a Growth Mindset: Embrace challenges and mistakes as opportunities for learning and growth. View setbacks as chances to develop new skills or improve your approach.

4. Take Responsibility:

- Own Your Actions: Clearly acknowledge your part in the situation. Use "I" statements to express your role and avoid defensiveness. For example, say, "I didn't meet the deadline because I mismanaged my time," rather than blaming external factors.

- Make Amends: If your actions have negatively impacted others, apologize and take steps to make things right. This demonstrates accountability and a willingness to improve.

5. Develop Problem-Solving Skills:

- Identify Actionable Steps: Determine concrete steps you can take to address the issue and prevent similar situations in the future. Focus on what you can control and influence.

- Create an Action Plan: Develop a plan with specific goals and actions to resolve the current problem and avoid future issues. Track your progress and make adjustments as needed.

6. Practice Self-Reflection:

- Regularly Reflect on Your Behavior: Take time to reflect on your actions and decisions. Consider journaling or discussing your reflections with a mentor or therapist.

- Seek Feedback: Ask for constructive feedback from others to gain different perspectives on your behavior and its impact. Use this feedback to identify areas for improvement.

7. Build Emotional Intelligence:

- Improve Self-Awareness: Work on understanding your emotions and how they influence your behavior. Techniques like mindfulness and emotional check-ins can be helpful.

- Enhance Self-Regulation: Practice managing your emotions and reactions. Techniques such as deep breathing, mindfulness, and cognitive restructuring can aid this process.

8. Foster Accountability:

- Set Personal Goals: Establish goals for taking ownership of various aspects of your life. Monitor your progress and hold yourself accountable for achieving these goals.

- Celebrate Successes: Acknowledge and celebrate your successes in taking ownership and resolving issues. Recognize the positive outcomes of your efforts.

9. Learn from Mistakes:

- Analyze Mistakes: When things don't go as planned, analyze what went wrong and why. Identify lessons learned and how you can apply them to future situations.

- Embrace Learning: Approach mistakes as opportunities for growth rather than failures. Use the insights gained to improve your approach and decision-making.

- 10. Seek Support if Needed:

- Consider Therapy or Coaching: If you find it challenging to shift from blaming to taking ownership, working with a therapist or coach can provide guidance and support.

- Join Support Groups: Engaging in support groups can offer additional perspectives and strategies for taking ownership and addressing challenges.

Exercises: Blame vs. Responsibility Worksheet: Identify patterns of blaming and how to shift towards taking responsibility.

Exercise 4.1

Objective: To identify when you're blaming others or external factors and shift your focus to taking responsibility for your emotions, actions, and decisions.

Step 1: Identify the Situation

Think of a recent situation where you felt frustrated, upset, or challenged. Write it down below.

Example Situation:

"I missed a deadline at work because I didn't plan my time properly."

Your Situation:

____

____

Step 2: Identify Blaming Thoughts

In this situation, did you find yourself blaming someone else or external circumstances for the issue? Write down any blaming thoughts that came to mind.

Example Blaming Thoughts:

"It's my boss's fault for not giving me enough time."
"The project was too complicated, so I couldn't finish on time."

Your Blaming Thoughts:

____

____

Step 3: Reflect on the Blame

For each blaming thought, ask yourself the following questions:

1.   Is this blame directed at someone else or external factors?
2.   What role did I play in this situation?

3. Could I have done something differently to improve the outcome?

Example Reflection for Blaming Thought:

Blaming Thought: *"It's my boss's fault for not giving me enough time."*

Reflection: I could have communicated earlier about my workload or asked for help prioritizing tasks.

Your Reflection for Blaming Thoughts:

1. **Blaming Thought:**

   ____

   Reflection:

   ____

2. **Blaming Thought:**

   ____

   Reflection:

   ____

3. **Blaming Thought:**

   ____

   Reflection:

   ____

Step 4: Shift to Responsibility

Now, reframe each blaming thought by shifting from blame to taking responsibility. This means acknowledging your part in the situation and focusing on what you can control and change.

Example Reframe:

Blaming: *"It's my boss's fault for not giving me enough time."*

Taking Responsibility: *"I didn't manage my time well and could have communicated my concerns earlier."*

Your Reframed Thoughts:

1. **Blaming Thought:**

   ____

   Reframe to Responsibility:

   ____

2. **Blaming Thought:**

   ____

   Reframe to Responsibility:

   ____

3. **Blaming Thought:**

   ____

   Reframe to Responsibility:

   ____

Step 5: Action Plan

Now that you've taken responsibility, think about the actions you can take to prevent this from happening again. What can you do differently next time to improve the situation?

Example Action Plan:

"Next time, I will prioritize my tasks more effectively and communicate with my boss if I feel the workload is overwhelming."

Your Action Plan:

____

____

____

Step 6: Reflect on the Process

Take a moment to reflect on how shifting from blame to responsibility feels. Does it change how you view the situation? How does it affect your emotions and actions?

Reflection:

"Shifting from blaming to taking responsibility makes me feel more empowered. I now see that I have control over my actions and can make improvements moving forward."

Summary & Takeaway:

By identifying patterns of blame and shifting towards responsibility, you take back your personal power. This not only fosters emotional maturity but also helps in building more constructive responses to challenges. With practice, you can reframe situations more quickly and move towards positive change.

Accountability Goals: Set practical goals for accepting and acting on feedback.

Objective: To set practical and actionable goals for accepting and acting on feedback in a constructive way.

Exercise 4.2

Step 1: Reflect on Recent Feedback

Think of a recent situation where you received feedback (positive or constructive). This could be from a colleague, supervisor, friend, or family member. Write down the feedback you received.

Example Feedback:

"You're doing great, but it would help if you could communicate your progress more often on the project."

Your Feedback:

____

____

____

Step 2: Acknowledge Your Initial Reaction

Reflect on how you felt when you received the feedback. Did you feel defensive, motivated, confused, or open? Write down your initial emotional reaction.

Example Reaction:

"I felt a little defensive at first because I thought I was doing enough. But I realized that communicating more clearly could help improve the project."

Your Emotional Reaction:

Step 3: Define Accountability Goals

Now that you've reflected on the feedback and your initial reaction, set clear, practical goals for how you can accept, and act on this feedback moving forward. These goals should be specific, measurable, and actionable.

Example Accountability Goals:

"I will set a reminder to update my team every Monday on my project progress."

"I will ask for clarification when receiving feedback to ensure I fully understand it."

Your Accountability Goals:

Step 4: Identify Potential Obstacles and Solutions

Think about any challenges you might face in following through with your goals. What might make it hard to act on the feedback, and how can you overcome these obstacles?

Example Obstacles:

"I might forget to send updates regularly."

Solution: "I'll set a recurring weekly reminder on my phone."

Your Obstacles and Solutions:

1. **Obstacles:**

   ____

   Solutions:

   ____

2. **Obstacles:**

   ____

   Solutions:

   ____

3. **Obstacles:**

   ____

   Solutions:

   ____

Step 5: Commit to Action

Finally, commit to taking action on your goals. Write down when you will start working on these goals and how you will track your progress.

Example Commitment:

"I'll start sending weekly updates next Monday, and I'll track my progress using a to-do list."

Your Commitment:

____

____

____

Step 6: Reflection & Accountability Check

Set a reminder for yourself to reflect on your progress after one week or after a specific time frame. Check in to see how well you've implemented the feedback and whether you've followed through on your accountability goals.

Reflection Questions:

- *"Have I been consistent in applying the feedback?"*
- *"What improvements have I noticed in my performance or relationships?"*
- *"What further adjustments can I make?"*

Next Check-In Date:

____

____

Summary:

By turning feedback into clear, actionable goals, you take responsibility for your growth and development. Regularly reviewing your progress and adjusting as needed ensures that you continue to improve and stay accountable to yourself and others.

Chapter 5

Facing Fear and Identifying Fallacies

Fear is a powerful force. It can stop you in your tracks, paralyze you with doubt, and keep you trapped in patterns of avoidance. But fear is often not as real as it feels. More often than not, it's based on fallacies—distorted beliefs and irrational thoughts that twist reality into something unrecognizable. Fear convinces you that the worst-case scenario is inevitable, that asking for help will make you weak or expose your vulnerability in ways that could shatter you. It tells you that failure is final, that you're not worthy of support, or that if you just try harder, you'll figure it out on your own.

In truth, fear and fallacies are two sides of the same coin. Fear thrives on uncertainty and exaggeration, distorting situations until they seem more dangerous, more overwhelming, and more permanent than they actually are. Identifying these fallacies—the exaggerated stories we tell ourselves about who we are, what we're capable of, and what the world expects of us—is one of the most liberating things we can do. When you can separate fact from fiction and face the irrational thoughts that fear feeds you, you start to see things more clearly. You start to recognize that many of the things you feared were never truly threats at all but just stories you'd been telling yourself for far too long.

This is where the real shift begins. Facing fear doesn't mean eliminating it. Fear is a natural part of being human, and it will always exist to some degree. But when you can identify the fallacies that fuel it—the lies you've internalized about being "too much" or "not enough"—you start to regain control over it. And that control is essential when it comes to asking for help.

Because here's the thing: fear and fallacies are at the heart of why most people struggle to ask for help. We tell ourselves that asking for help means admitting weakness, that it will make us a burden, or that it will expose our inadequacies to the people around us. But that's a fallacy. Asking for help is not a sign of weakness; it's a sign of courage and self-awareness. It's the realization that we are not meant to carry the weight of the world alone. Fear of judgment, fear of rejection, and fear of being seen as "less than" are all rooted in fallacies—distorted beliefs that keep us isolated in our suffering.

When you face those fears and confront the false beliefs they create, you allow yourself the space to be human. You allow yourself to say,

"I don't have to do this alone," and "It's okay to ask for help." It's through this process of facing fear and identifying fallacies that we become more connected to ourselves and to others. Only when we recognize that much of what we fear is not rooted in reality can we begin to move past it and step into the support and growth that asking for help brings.

Objective: Address fears associated with asking for help and recognize cognitive distortions.

Facing fears and identifying fallacies of thought involves understanding and challenging the irrational or distorted ways you might be thinking and actively confronting the fears that these thoughts often fuel. Here's a structured approach to help you manage and overcome these challenges:

1. Face Your Fears:

1.1. Identify Your Fears:

- **List Your Fears:** Write down specific fears that you have. Be as detailed as possible. For example, if you fear public speaking, specify whether it's the fear of being judged, making a mistake, or forgetting what to say.
- **Assess the Impact:** Reflect on how these fears are affecting your life. Are they preventing you from pursuing opportunities or engaging in activities you enjoy?

1.2. Understand the Root Causes:

- **Explore Origins:** Consider where these fears might have originated. Did a specific experience or event contribute to your current fears?

- **Analyze Triggers:** Identify what situations, thoughts, or feelings trigger your fears. Understanding triggers can help you prepare for and manage them.

1.3. Gradual Exposure:

- **Start Small:** Begin by exposing yourself to your fears in small, manageable ways. For example, if you fear public speaking, start by speaking in small, informal settings.

- **Increase Gradually:** Gradually increase the level of exposure as you build confidence. This can help desensitize you to the fear and make it less overwhelming.

1.4. Use Relaxation Techniques:

- **Practice Mindfulness:** Engage in mindfulness or meditation practices to manage anxiety and stay grounded when facing your fears.

- **Employ Breathing Exercises:** Use deep breathing techniques to calm your nervous system and reduce the physiological symptoms of fear.

2. Identify and Challenge Fallacies of Thought:

2.1. Recognize Cognitive Distortions:

- **Common Distortions:** Familiarize yourself with common cognitive distortions such as catastrophizing (expecting the worst), black-and-white thinking (seeing things as all good or all bad), or overgeneralization (making broad conclusions based on limited evidence).

- **Identify Your Patterns:** Pay attention to when and how these distortions occur in your thinking. Notice if they are more prevalent during stressful situations or specific types of problems.

2.2. Challenge Distorted Thoughts:

- **Examine Evidence:** Assess the evidence for and against your distorted thoughts. Ask yourself whether there is factual evidence supporting your negative beliefs or if they are based on assumptions.

- **Reframe Your Thoughts:** Replace distorted thoughts with more balanced and realistic ones. For instance, if you're thinking, "I always fail," reframe it to, "I have faced challenges before, but I have also succeeded."

2.3. Use Thought Records:

- **Document Your Thoughts:** Keep a thought record to track and analyze your automatic thoughts. Write down the situation, thoughts, emotions, and alternative, more balanced thoughts.

- **Review and Reflect:** Regularly review your thought records to identify patterns and evaluate how your alternative thoughts affect your emotions and behavior.

2.4. Apply Problem-Solving Techniques:

- **Break Down Issues:** When faced with a problem, break it down into smaller, manageable parts. Address each part separately to avoid feeling overwhelmed.

- **Generate Solutions:** Develop a list of potential solutions to the problems you're facing. Evaluate the pros and cons of each solution and choose the most effective one.

2.5. Seek Feedback and Support:

- **Talk to Others:** Discuss your fears and distorted thoughts with trusted friends, family members, or a therapist. They can provide valuable perspectives and help you challenge irrational beliefs.

- **Consider Professional Help:** A therapist trained in cognitive-behavioral therapy (CBT) can provide guidance in identifying and addressing cognitive distortions and fears.

3. Integrate New Strategies:

3.1. Practice Self-Compassion:

- **Be Kind to Yourself:** Treat yourself with kindness and understanding. Recognize that everyone experiences fears and distorted thoughts, and it's part of being human.

- **Acknowledge Progress:** Celebrate your successes in facing fears and challenging distorted thoughts, no matter how small. Recognize and appreciate the progress you're making.

3.2. Maintain Consistent Practice:

- **Regular Review:** Continuously review and apply the strategies for facing fears and challenging distortions. Consistency helps reinforce new, healthier thought patterns and behaviors.

- **Adapt Strategies:** Adjust your approach as needed based on your experiences and progress. Be flexible and open to trying new techniques if you find certain strategies more effective.

Conclusion:

Facing fears and identifying fallacies of thought requires self-awareness, patience, and practice. By understanding your fears, gradually exposing yourself to them, and challenging cognitive distortions, you can build resilience and develop healthier, more balanced thinking patterns. Seeking support from professionals and engaging in consistent practice can further enhance your ability to manage and overcome these challenges.

Exercises 5.1: Fear Exploration: List and explore your fears related to seeking help.

Exercise 5.2 Fallacies Identification: Spot common fallacies in your thinking and challenge them.

Objective: To help you identify cognitive distortions (thought fallacies) in your thinking and begin shifting toward more realistic, balanced thoughts.

Step 1: Review Common Thought Fallacies

Here are some of the most common cognitive distortions. Take a moment to familiarize yourself with them:

- **All-or-Nothing Thinking**: Seeing situations in black-and-white terms, with no middle ground. ("If I don't do this perfectly, I've failed.")

- **Overgeneralization**: Making broad, sweeping conclusions based on one or a few events. ("I failed this project, so I'll never succeed.")

- **Mental Filter**: Focusing only on the negative aspects of a situation and ignoring any positives. ("I made one mistake during the presentation, so it was a disaster.")

- **Discounting the Positive**: Dismissing positive experiences or accomplishments as insignificant. ("That compliment doesn't count; they were just being nice.")

- **Jumping to Conclusions**: Making assumptions without evidence, like mind reading or predicting the future. ("They didn't text me back; they must be angry with me.")

- **Catastrophizing**: Expecting the worst possible outcome. ("If I don't get this job, my career is over.")

- **Personalization**: Blaming yourself for things outside of your control. ("If my team failed, it's my fault.")

- **Emotional Reasoning**: Believing that because you feel something, it must be true. ("I feel anxious, so something bad is going to happen.")

- **Should Statements**: Using "should," "must," or "ought" statements that create unrealistic expectations for yourself or others. ("I should always be happy and calm.")

- **Labeling**: Assigning a negative label to yourself or others based on one behavior or event. ("I made a mistake; I'm such a failure.")

Step 2: Identify a Recent Situation

Think about a recent situation where you felt upset, stressed, or frustrated. Write down a specific event or challenge you faced.

Example Situation:

"I received some constructive feedback at work about my presentation."

Your Situation:

____

____

____

Step 3: Recognize the Thought Fallacies

In the situation you wrote down, what automatic thoughts did you have? Try to identify which thought fallacies might be influencing your perception.

Example Thoughts and Fallacies:

"The feedback was really harsh. I'll never get this right."

Fallacy: **All-or-Nothing Thinking** (viewing feedback as all negative)

"My manager probably thinks I'm not good enough."

Fallacy: **Mind Reading** (assuming what others think without evidence)

Your Thoughts and Fallacies:

1. **Thoughts:**

    ____

    Fallacies:

    ____

2. **Thoughts:**

    ____

    Fallacies:

    ____

3. **Thoughts:**

    ____

    Fallacies:

    ____

Step 4: Challenge the Distorted Thoughts

Now, challenge each of the thought fallacies you've identified. Ask yourself:

- What evidence do I have for and against this thought?
- What's a more balanced or realistic way to think about this situation?
- How would I view this situation if I were being kinder to myself?

Example Challenge for All-or-Nothing Thinking:

Original Thought: *"I'll never get this right."*

Balanced Reframe: *"I received constructive feedback, and I can use it to improve. I don't have to be perfect, but I can always get better."*

Your Challenges and Reframes:

1. **Original Thoughts:**

   ____

   Balanced Reframe:

   ____

2. **Original Thoughts:**

   ____

   Balanced Reframe:

   ____

3. **Original Thoughts:**

   ____

   Balanced Reframe:

   ____

Step 5: Reflect on the Impact

After reframing your thoughts, reflect on how this new perspective might change your emotional response and behavior.

Example Reflection:

"By shifting my thinking, I feel less stressed and more motivated to improve based on the feedback. I don't feel like a failure anymore."

Your Reflection:

"By challenging my thoughts, I feel more empowered to handle the situation without unnecessary stress. I can take action and learn from it."

Summary:

Recognizing and challenging thought fallacies helps you break free from negative thinking patterns and cultivate a more balanced mindset. By practicing this exercise regularly, you can improve emotional resilience and make more rational decisions in the face of challenges.

Trust vs. Mistrust – Building Healthy Relationships

Trust is the foundation of every meaningful connection we have in life. It's the belief that, when we reach out, we will be met with understanding, support, and care—whether in a family, friendship, or professional relationship. Trust allows us to be vulnerable and to share our fears, our dreams, and our struggles with others, knowing they will meet us with empathy and respect. It's the invisible thread that binds people together, creating bonds of safety and mutual support. Without trust, relationships crumble. Walls go up, communication breaks down, and the heart of connection is lost.

But what happens when trust is absent? When the foundation is cracked or nonexistent? That's when mistrust takes root, a silent poison that shapes how we see others and ourselves. Mistrust tells us that people can't be relied upon, that we are alone in our struggles, and that asking for help is risky. Mistrust builds walls, reinforces isolation, and makes every request for support feel like an act of vulnerability that could be met with rejection, judgment, or betrayal. It's a toxic belief system that skews our perceptions, causing us to withdraw, avoid connection, and handle everything ourselves—even when we're drowning.

Consider the image of a fox caught in a bear trap. It struggles in the steel jaws of its imprisonment, desperate to escape, but its pain and fear are compounded by a deep mistrust. The trap has been set by a hunter—the same person who holds the key to releasing it. But the fox, in its panic, cannot see that the hunter might offer help. All it knows is that the hunter is a source of danger, not salvation. The fox, unable to trust that the hunter will release it, keeps chewing at its own leg, thinking only of escape through pain, unaware that the one who can help is standing just outside its line of sight.

This mistrust mirrors how we sometimes react when stuck in our emotional traps. When we're caught in the struggles of life—whether it's the weight of past trauma, a struggle with addiction, or feelings of isolation—we often mistrust the people around us. We assume that if we ask for help, we'll only be hurt or rejected. We may have been let down in the past or internalized the belief that we are unworthy of support. Like the fox, we see the hand reaching out to help us, but instead of trusting it, we push it away, convinced that we are better off suffering alone.

But here's the truth: mistrust, while often rooted in past pain, keeps us trapped in our own suffering. Just as the fox cannot free itself from the trap alone, we cannot heal, grow, or move forward without the support of others. And just like the hunter, the people who are ready and willing to help us may not always look the way we expect them to. They might not be perfect or have all the answers, but their support is the key to our release.

Learning to build trust—first with ourselves and then with others—is the first step toward emotional freedom. It means recognizing that not everyone who reaches out is an enemy and that asking for help doesn't make us weak or unworthy but human. Trust isn't a simple switch that can be flipped overnight, but it is something we can build over time through consistent actions and honest vulnerability. As we learn to trust, we begin to see that asking for help isn't a sign of failure but a vital part of the healing process. It's the very thing that will help us free ourselves from the traps we've been caught in.

Objective: Explore issues of trust and mistrust and how they impact your ability to seek help.

The concept of "trust versus mistrust" originates from Erik Erikson's psychosocial development theory, specifically from the first stage of development. This stage is crucial as it forms the foundation for how individuals perceive and interact with the world throughout their lives. Here's an explanation of the concept and how to build healthy relationships based on it:

Trust vs. Mistrust:

1. Understanding the Concept:

- **Definition:** In Erikson's theory, the trust vs. mistrust stage occurs from birth to about 18 months. It involves an infant's developing sense of trust or mistrust based on their interactions with caregivers and their environment.

- **Trust:** When caregivers consistently provide care, warmth, and comfort, infants develop a sense of trust and security. They learn that they can depend on others and that the world is safe.

- **Mistrust:** Conversely, if caregivers are inconsistent, neglectful, or abusive, infants may develop mistrust. They may view the world as unreliable and dangerous, impacting their future relationships and emotional well-being.

2. Building Healthy Relationships Based on Trust vs. Mistrust:

2.1. Foster Trust in Yourself:

- **Self-Reflection:** Examine your own experiences and patterns related to trust and mistrust. Reflect on how your early experiences have shaped your beliefs and behaviors in relationships.

- **Self-Care:** Build self-trust by practicing self-care and setting healthy boundaries. Ensure that your needs are met and that you're treating yourself with kindness and respect.

2.2. Build Trust with Others:

- **Be Consistent:** Consistency in your actions and words helps build trust. Follow through on commitments, be reliable, and maintain integrity in your relationships.

- **Communicate Openly:** Open and honest communication is essential for building trust. Share your thoughts, feelings, and expectations clearly and listen actively to others.

- **Show Empathy:** Demonstrate understanding and compassion towards others. Validate their feelings and experiences and provide support when needed.

2.3. Address and Overcome Mistrust:

- **Identify Sources of Mistrust:** Recognize and address the underlying causes of mistrust. This might involve reflecting on past experiences or traumas that have influenced your current perceptions.

- **Challenge Negative Beliefs:** Work on challenging and reframing negative beliefs about trust. Replace irrational fears or generalizations with more balanced and realistic perspectives.

- **Gradual Exposure:** If you struggle with mistrust, gradually expose yourself to situations where trust can be built. Start with small, low-risk interactions and build up as you gain confidence.

2.4. Build and Maintain Healthy Relationships:

- **Establish Boundaries:** Set and respect boundaries in relationships. Clearly communicate your limits and be attentive to the boundaries of others.

- **Seek Mutual Respect:** Ensure relationships are based on mutual respect and understanding. Both parties should feel valued and heard.

- **Promote Reciprocity:** Build relationships on reciprocity, where both individuals contribute and benefit. Healthy relationships involve a balance of give and take.

2.5. Develop Emotional Intelligence:

- **Enhance Self-Awareness:** Develop a deeper understanding of your emotions and how they affect your interactions. Practice recognizing and managing your emotional responses.

- **Improve Social Skills:** Work on skills such as active listening, empathy, and conflict resolution. These skills foster positive interactions and strengthen relationships.

2.6. Seek Support When Needed:

- **Consider Therapy:** If past experiences of mistrust significantly impact your current relationships, therapy can help. A therapist can assist in processing past traumas and developing healthier relationship patterns.

- **Join Support Groups:** Engaging in support groups can provide additional perspectives and strategies for building trust and managing relationship challenges.

Conclusion:

The trust vs. mistrust stage sets the foundation for how individuals perceive and engage in relationships throughout their lives. By fostering self-trust, building consistent and empathetic relationships with others, and addressing and overcoming mistrust, you can cultivate healthier, more fulfilling connections. Developing emotional intelligence and seeking support when needed further enhances your ability to build and maintain trust in relationships.

Exercises 6.1: Trust Assessment: Reflect on past experiences that shaped your trust in others.

87

Exercise 6.2 Trust Building Strategies: Develop practical steps to build and maintain healthy relationships.

Objective: To develop practical steps for building trust and maintaining healthy relationships by fostering open communication, consistency, and mutual respect.

Step 1: Identify a Relationship to Focus On

Think of a relationship in your life where you'd like to build or strengthen trust. It could be with a partner, friend, colleague, or family member.

Example Relationship:

"I want to build trust with my colleague because we are working on a project together."

Your Relationship:

____

____

____

Step 2: Reflect on the Current State of Trust

How would you describe the current level of trust in this relationship? Are there any areas where trust is lacking or where you've experienced miscommunication, disappointment, or insecurity?

Example Reflection:

"There's a good foundation of trust, but I've noticed a few communication gaps when discussing project updates."

Your Reflection:

Step 3: Identify Specific Trust-Building Strategies

Think of practical steps you can take to strengthen trust in this relationship. Here are some strategies to consider:

1. **Consistent Communication:** Regularly check in with the other person and keep them informed about your thoughts, feelings, or actions.
2. **Honesty and Transparency:** Be open about your needs, concerns, and expectations, even if it's uncomfortable.
3. **Reliability and Dependability:** Follow through on promises and commitments. Be someone the other person can rely on.
4. **Active Listening:** Give the other person space to share their perspective and listen without judgment or interrupting.
5. **Respecting Boundaries:** Understand and honor the other person's needs, preferences, and limits.
6. **Apologizing and Making Amends:** When trust is broken, acknowledge your part and take steps to repair the situation.

Your Trust-Building Strategies:

____

____

____

Step 4: Commit to Action

Select one or two trust-building strategies that you can begin implementing right away. Write down your specific action steps and commit to them.

Example Action Plan:

"I will send weekly updates to my colleague on the project's progress to ensure clear communication."

"I will make a point of listening carefully and not interrupting when we meet to discuss the project."

Your Action Plan:

1. **Strategy:**

    ____

    Action:

    ____

2. **Strategy:**

    ____

    Action:

    ____

3. Strategy:

____

Action:

____

Step 5: Set a Check-In Date

After you've committed to these action steps, set a date for when you will check in with yourself to assess how things are going. This allows you to reflect on progress, adjust strategies if needed, and continue strengthening trust.

Example Check-In:

"I'll check in with myself in one month to assess how my communication with my colleague is improving."

Your Check-In Date:

____

____

____

Reflection Questions for Check-In:

- "What progress have I made in building trust?"
- "Have I noticed any positive changes in the relationship?"
- "Are there any areas where I need to adjust my approach?"

Step 6: Reflect on the Impact

Once you've implemented your trust-building strategies, reflect on how they have affected the relationship. Do you feel more connected and secure? How has the other person responded?

Example Reflection:

"By staying consistent with updates, my colleague feels more involved, and we've had fewer misunderstandings. I feel more confident about our project work."

Your Reflection:

____

____

____

Summary:

Building and maintaining trust requires intentional effort, communication, and consistency. By committing to practical trust-building strategies, you strengthen your relationships and create a foundation of mutual respect, understanding, and support.

Chapter 7

Overcoming Helplessness, Hopelessness, and Worthlessness

Helplessness, hopelessness, and worthlessness are three of the most insidious emotions we can experience. They rob us of our agency, our motivation, and our belief in a better future. These feelings are often the aftermath of trauma, rejection, or prolonged pain. And when they take hold, they can feel overwhelming—like a heavy weight pressing down on our chest, making it hard to breathe, think, or move forward.

Helplessness is the feeling that we have no control and that our actions and efforts are futile. It's the belief that no matter what we do, nothing will change. It keeps us stuck, unable to take the next step, because we feel paralyzed by the belief that we're powerless. This emotional paralysis often makes it impossible to reach out for help because we believe that nothing anyone can do will make a difference.

Hopelessness is the absence of expectation, the quiet belief that things will never get better, that no light can pierce the darkness we find ourselves in. It's the sense that no matter how hard we try, nothing we do will ever be enough to change our reality. Hopelessness tells us that the future is just a continuation of the present, filled with more pain, more struggle, and more disappointment. In this state, asking for help seems pointless because we believe no one can change the outcome, not even ourselves.

Worthlessness is the internalized belief that we are not enough and don't deserve help, love, or success. It's the voice inside our heads telling us that we're broken, unworthy, or fundamentally flawed. Worthlessness convinces us that asking for help is an admission of our inadequacy and that no one would want to help someone who doesn't deserve it in the first place.

These emotions—helplessness, hopelessness, and worthlessness—are all intertwined. They create a self-perpetuating cycle that keeps us isolated and stuck in patterns of self-doubt and despair. They prevent us from reaching out because they convince us that we're too small, too broken, or too insignificant to ask for help. They make it feel like the world is too big, too indifferent, and we are too small to matter.

Now, imagine a fox caught in a bear trap. The sharp steel jaws have closed around its leg, and every instinct in the fox screams to escape. But in its fear and pain, the fox becomes convinced that it's too late. It believes it has no way out—that the trap has already done its damage and's beyond saving. It pulls at its own leg, gnawing at the wound, convinced that it must endure the pain alone. The fox, feeling helpless, hopeless, and worthless in its current state, cannot see the possibility of someone—the hunter—coming to its aid. It believes that no one would help, that it's too late, or that it doesn't deserve help in the first place. The fox's suffering is compounded by its inability to trust, to ask for help, and to see the possibility of release.

This image of the trapped fox is not unlike how we feel when consumed by helplessness, hopelessness, and worthlessness. These emotions create a fog that obscures our ability to reach out, to see the hands extended toward us, and to believe that things can get better. We begin to think that we must handle everything on our own, that we don't deserve help, or that no one would want to help someone like us.

But just as the fox is not beyond rescue, we are never beyond help. Overcoming these feelings requires us to confront the lies they tell us. It means challenging the belief that we are powerless, that the future holds no hope, and that we are not worthy of kindness or care. The first step toward healing is recognizing that these feelings are not facts—they are distorted perceptions shaped by pain and fear. They are not truths about who we are but obstacles to seeing the truth of our worth and potential.

In this chapter, we will explore how to break free from helplessness, hopelessness, and worthlessness. We will learn how to open ourselves up to help, how to recognize the value of our own lives, and how to rebuild the belief that asking for help is not a sign of weakness but a step toward healing. Just as the fox must learn to trust the hand of the hunter for release, we must learn to trust that support is available, that help is possible, and that we are always worthy of both.

Objective: Address feelings of helplessness, hopelessness, and worthlessness that may impede your ability to seek help.

Feeling helpless, hopeless, and worthless can be overwhelming and paralyzing, often leading to difficulties in seeking help. These feelings can create a barrier to reaching out for support due to various psychological and emotional factors. Here's why these feelings can inhibit help-seeking and how to overcome them:

Why These Feelings Inhibit Seeking Help:

1. Helplessness:

- **Belief in Ineffectiveness:** If you feel helpless, you might believe that nothing you do will make a difference, making seeking help seem futile.

- **Fear of Burdening Others:** Feeling helpless can lead to the fear that asking for help will burden or inconvenience others, reinforcing the idea that you should handle everything on your own.

- **Lack of Control:** Helplessness often involves a sense of losing control over your life. Seeking help might feel like giving up more control or admitting defeat.

2. Hopelessness:

- **Pessimism About Change:** When you feel hopeless, you may be convinced that things will never get better. This pessimism can prevent you from believing that seeking help could lead to positive change.

- **Disconnection from Solutions:** Hopelessness can create a disconnection from potential solutions. You might feel that no intervention or assistance could alleviate your situation.

- **Emotional Exhaustion:** Hopelessness often comes with emotional exhaustion, making it difficult to muster the energy or motivation to seek help.

3. Worthlessness:

- **Low Self-Esteem:** Feeling worthless can lead to believing that you don't deserve help or that others wouldn't value or understand your struggles.

- **Shame and Guilt:** Worthlessness can bring about feelings of shame or guilt, making it challenging to seek help because you may feel unworthy or like a burden.

- **Fear of Rejection:** If you feel worthless, you might fear that seeking help will result in rejection or judgment, reinforcing the belief that you're not deserving of support.

How to Overcome These Barriers:

1. Challenge and Reframe Negative Beliefs:

- **Identify and Question Beliefs:** Recognize negative beliefs associated with helplessness, hopelessness, and worthlessness. Challenge these beliefs by asking yourself whether they are based on facts or distorted thinking.

- **Reframe Perspectives:** Replace negative thoughts with more balanced, realistic ones. For instance, instead of thinking, "Nothing will ever change," try "Seeking help might lead to improvements, even if I can't see how right now."

2. Set Small, Achievable Goals:

- **Break Down Tasks:** Set small, manageable goals for reaching out for help. For example, starting by talking to a trusted friend or researching local resources can be less intimidating than seeking professional help immediately.

- **Celebrate Progress:** Recognize and celebrate even small steps toward seeking help. Acknowledging these achievements can build confidence and motivation.

3. Build a Support Network:

- **Reach Out to Trusted Individuals:** Connect with friends, family, or support groups who can offer understanding and encouragement. Having a support system can make seeking help feel less daunting.

- **Engage in Community Resources:** Utilize community resources such as support groups, hotlines, or online forums where you can connect with others who understand your experiences.

4. Practice Self-Compassion:

- **Treat Yourself Kindly:** Practice self-compassion by being kind to yourself and recognizing that everyone struggles with difficult feelings at times. Avoid self-criticism and offer yourself the same support you would give to a friend.

- **Acknowledge Your Strengths:** Reflect on your strengths and past achievements. Recognizing your value and abilities can help counteract feelings of worthlessness.

5. Seek Professional Help:

- **Therapy and Counseling:** Consider seeking help from a mental health professional. Therapy can provide a safe space to explore and address feelings of helplessness, hopelessness, and worthlessness.

- **Medication:** In some cases, medication prescribed by a healthcare provider can help manage symptoms of depression and anxiety, making it easier to engage in therapeutic processes.

6. Develop Coping Strategies:

- **Practice Mindfulness:** Engage in mindfulness or meditation practices to stay present and manage negative thoughts. These techniques can help reduce emotional distress and increase self-awareness.

- **Use Coping Skills:** Develop and use coping skills such as journaling, exercise, or relaxation techniques to manage stress and emotional challenges.

7. Educate Yourself:

- **Learn About Mental Health:** Educate yourself about mental health issues and treatments. Understanding that feelings of helplessness, hopelessness, and worthlessness are common and treatable can reduce stigma and increase motivation to seek help.

- **Explore Self-Help Resources:** Access self-help books, online resources, or workshops that provide tools and strategies for managing negative emotions and building resilience.

Conclusion:

Overcoming feelings of helplessness, hopelessness, and worthlessness involves challenging negative beliefs, setting small goals, and building a supportive network. Practicing self-compassion and seeking professional help are also crucial steps. By addressing these feelings and taking proactive measures, you can gradually build the confidence and motivation needed to seek the help and support you deserve.

Exercise 7.1: Helplessness Inventory: Identify areas where you feel helpless and explore alternative perspectives.

Objective: To identify areas where you feel helpless and to explore alternative perspectives that can help you regain a sense of empowerment and control.

Step 1: Reflect on Areas of Helplessness

Think of a few situations in your life where you feel helpless, stuck, or unable to progress. These might involve work, relationships, personal goals, or emotional challenges. Write down at least 2-3 areas where you often feel powerless.

Example Areas of Helplessness:

"I feel helpless in my job because I don't have control over the projects I get assigned."

"I feel stuck in my relationship because we keep having the same arguments without resolution."

"I feel overwhelmed by my personal goals because I don't know where to start."

Your Areas of Helplessness:

____

____

____

Step 2: Explore Your Current Thoughts and Feelings

For each area you listed, write down the automatic thoughts and feelings that come up when you think about the situation. How do these thoughts reinforce your sense of helplessness? What emotions arise (e.g., frustration, hopelessness, anxiety)?

Example Reflection:

"When I think about my job, I feel frustrated and think, 'No matter how hard I try, I can't change anything.'"

"In my relationship, I feel hopeless and think, 'We'll never get past these issues.'"

Your Thoughts and Feelings:

1. **Area 1:**

   Thoughts: ____

   Feelings: ____

2. **Area 2:**

   Thoughts: ____

   Feelings: ____

3. **Area 3:**

   Thoughts: ____

   Feelings: ____

Step 3: Identify Patterns of Helplessness

Now, try to identify any patterns in your thinking. Do you notice a tendency to catastrophize, overgeneralize, or assume that things are beyond your control? Write down any recurring cognitive patterns that contribute to the sense of helplessness.

Example Patterns:

"I tend to believe that because I can't change the big things, I can't make any difference at all."

"I often assume that things won't improve, so I avoid taking action."

Your Patterns of Helplessness:

Step 4: Reframe Your Perspective

Now, for each area where you feel helpless, try to shift your perspective to one of empowerment. What alternative, more balanced, realistic thoughts can you replace your helpless thoughts with? Focus on what **you can control** in each situation, even if it's just your response or your actions.

Example Reframing:

"I may not control the projects I get assigned, but I can communicate my preferences and take ownership of my work to the best of my ability."

"We may have recurring issues in our relationship, but I can take the first step toward resolving them by initiating a calm conversation or seeking couples' counseling."

Your Reframed Thoughts:

1. **Area 1:**
   Helpless Thought: _______________________________

   Reframed Thought: _______________________________

2. **Area 2:**
   Helpless Thought: _______________________________

   Reframed Thought: _______________________________

3. **Area 3:**
   Helpless Thought: _______________________________

   Reframed Thought: _______________________________

Step 5: Identify Concrete Actions You Can Take

For each area, identify one concrete action you can take to begin moving away from helplessness and toward more empowerment. This could be something small or simple that will help you regain a sense of control and progress.

Example Actions:

"I'll talk to my manager about my role and see if there's an opportunity for me to take on more projects that align with my skills."

"I'll have a calm conversation with my partner about how we can work together to resolve our issues."

Your Concrete Actions:

1. **Area 1 Action:** _______________________________

2. **Area 2 Action:** _______________________________

3. **Area 3 Action:** _______________________________

Step 6: Reflection and Reassessment

After taking action, revisit this exercise in a few weeks or months. How has your perspective shifted? Do you still feel helpless in these areas, or have you found a way to regain control and take positive steps forward?

Reflection:

"By focusing on what I can control, I feel more empowered. I've taken a few steps toward resolving my challenges and feel less stuck."

"I realized that even small actions can help improve my situation and give me more confidence in managing challenges."

Summary:

This **Helplessness Inventory** helps you recognize when you're feeling powerless, explore the underlying thoughts that contribute to this feeling, and reframe those thoughts to focus on what you **can** control. By taking small, practical steps toward change, you can regain a sense of agency and start shifting away from helplessness.

Exercise 7.2: Hope Cultivation: Practice exercises to foster a sense of hope and possibility.

Objective: To practice exercises that help you nurture hope, increase optimism, and create a vision for your future filled with possibility and action.

Step 1: Reflect on a Past Success

Think of a time in your life when you overcame a challenge, achieved a goal, or felt a sense of accomplishment. This could be anything, big or small, that you are proud of. Reflect on this success to remind yourself that positive change is possible.

Example Reflection:

"I was able to complete a difficult project at work, even though I initially doubted my ability to succeed."

Your Past Success:

- What did you achieve?

  ____

- How did it feel to succeed in this area?

  ____

Step 2: Identify Strengths That Helped You Succeed

Now, think about the strengths, skills, or resources that helped you achieve that success. What qualities did you rely on? This exercise helps you recognize the inner resources you have to handle challenges and create hope for future possibilities.

Example Strengths:

"I was persistent, and I asked for help when I needed it. My creativity also helped me find solutions to problems."

Your Strengths:

____

____

____

Step 3: Envision a Positive Future

Imagine a future situation where you feel hopeful and excited about what lies ahead. What does this future look like? Take a few moments to visualize a future where you have overcome current obstacles and achieved your goals. Try to picture as many details as possible.

Example Future Vision:

"I see myself in a career I love, feeling confident in my abilities and constantly learning. I have healthy, supportive relationships, and I feel fulfilled in my personal and professional life."

Your Future Vision:

____

____

Step 4: Identify Small Action Steps to Create Hope

What is one small action you can take today or in the near future to bring you closer to the positive future you've visualized? The goal is to take a concrete step to create momentum toward the possibilities you envision.

Example Action Step:

"I will reach out to a mentor to discuss my career goals and ask for advice on transitioning to a role I'm passionate about."

Your Action Step:

____

____

Step 5: Focus on a Positive Affirmation

Choose a positive affirmation that reinforces hope and possibility in your life. This could be a simple statement like, "I am capable of overcoming challenges" or "I trust that positive opportunities are ahead." Write it down and repeat it to yourself daily to keep your mindset focused on possibility.

Example Affirmation:

"Every step I take, no matter how small, brings me closer to my goals."

Your Affirmation:

____

____

Step 6: Set a Hopeful Check-In Date

Commit to revisiting this exercise in a week or two. At that time, check in with yourself about how you've followed through with your action step, how your perspective on hope has evolved, and what other steps you can take to keep fostering hope in your life.

Example Check-In Date:

"I'll check in with myself in two weeks to see how my conversation with my mentor went and assess what progress I've made toward my career goals."

Your Check-In Date:

____

____

____

Reflection Questions for Check-In:

- "What progress have I made toward my goal?"
- "How has my sense of hope and possibility grown?"
- "What's the next small action step I can take?"

Summary:

By reflecting on past successes, identifying strengths, visualizing a positive future, and taking concrete action, you cultivate hope and possibility in your life. This exercise helps you shift from feelings of uncertainty to optimism and motivation, guiding you toward positive change.

Chapter 8

Enhancing Self-Worth and Addressing Worthlessness

There is nothing more crippling than the belief that you are unworthy. Worthlessness is a deep, painful conviction that infects every part of your being. It's the voice that whispers you're not good enough, that you don't deserve love, success, or even basic care. It distorts how you see yourself, how you interact with others, and, most importantly, how you navigate the world. When worthlessness takes root, it clouds your judgment, turns every struggle into a confirmation of your inadequacy, and convinces you that asking for help is a betrayal of your unworthiness.

Worthlessness does more than harm your self-image—it undermines your mental health. It feeds directly into the cycles of anxiety and depression, creating a constant, heavy fog that makes it hard to find clarity, hope, or motivation. Anxiety tells you that you're never enough, that you're always falling short or waiting for the other shoe to drop. Depression convinces you that you're too broken to be fixed, that life will never change, and that your pain is permanent. Together, these mental battles build a fortress of isolation, reinforcing the belief that you're not worthy of support or even relief.

In many ways, worthlessness is a barrier—an invisible wall that keeps you locked inside your own mind, unwilling or unable to reach out for the help you so desperately need. When you feel unworthy, the idea of asking for help becomes foreign, even impossible. It's as if you're trying to reach for something you believe you don't deserve or can't attain. In those moments, the thought of being vulnerable and opening up to someone else feels like a violation because you are still convinced that you're not worthy of their time, care, or attention.

Imagine, for a moment, the fox in the bear trap. Its leg is ensnared, bloodied, and trapped in the cold jaws of the trap. The fox is suffering, and every instinct tells it to escape, to break free of the pain. But in its mind, the trap is final—there's no way out, no one who would help, no reason to hope. The fox feels worthless in its struggle. It's too broken to be saved, too far gone to ever be free. It doesn't trust that anyone—especially the hunter standing just out of sight—will come to its aid. Its belief in its own unworthiness keeps it trapped in isolation, gnawing at its own leg, even though the potential for freedom lies just beyond its reach.

This is how worthlessness works—it distorts our reality, clouds our ability to see the support around us, and keeps us from the very things that can heal us. The fox's suffering isn't just physical; it's emotional and psychological, much like our own battles with self-worth. When we feel worthless, we cannot see the possibility of a better life or the hands reaching out to help us. We pull back, unsure that we deserve it, unsure that anyone could or would want to help someone like us. And so we continue to struggle, feeling stuck, unseen, and unworthy of anything better.

To overcome this, we must begin the difficult but vital task of addressing worthlessness head-on. It means unlearning the false beliefs that tell us we are unworthy. It means challenging the negative stories we've internalized about who we are and replacing them with truths that affirm our inherent value. You are not defined by your mistakes, your flaws, or your struggles. You are defined by your humanity, your capacity for growth, and your worth as a person— not just because of what you can offer others but because you exist.

In this chapter, we will explore practical steps to enhance your self-worth and break free from the grip of worthlessness that feeds your anxiety and depression. We'll look at how addressing these deep-seated beliefs about yourself can begin to shift the way you perceive the world and, more importantly, yourself. As you challenge the lies of worthlessness, you'll see that you deserve help. You are worthy of love and support. Most importantly, you'll begin to understand that asking for help is not a weakness but a powerful act of self-recognition. It's the first step in healing, in reclaiming your worth, and in stepping into the life you were always meant to lead.

Objective: Boost your sense of self-worth and counteract feelings of worthlessness.

Enhancing self-worth is a multifaceted process that involves developing a positive self-image, building confidence, and cultivating self-compassion. Here's a structured approach to help you enhance your self-worth:

1. Recognize and Challenge Negative Self-Beliefs:

1.1. Identify Negative Beliefs:

- **Self-Reflection:** Pay attention to recurring negative thoughts about yourself. Notice any patterns or specific areas where you feel unworthy.

- **Journaling:** Write down these negative beliefs and explore their origins. This can help you understand why you hold these beliefs and how they impact your self-worth.

1.2. Challenge and Reframe:

- **Evaluate Evidence:** Assess whether these negative beliefs are based on facts or distortions. Challenge these beliefs by considering evidence that contradicts them.

- **Reframe Thoughts:** Replace negative beliefs with more balanced and positive ones. For example, instead of thinking, "I'm not good enough," reframe it to, "I have unique strengths and qualities."

2. Set and Achieve Personal Goals:

2.1. Set Realistic Goals:

- **Identify Objectives:** Set clear, achievable goals that align with your values and interests. Break these goals into smaller, manageable steps.

- **Create an Action Plan:** Develop a plan for achieving your goals, including specific actions, deadlines, and resources needed.

2.2. Celebrate Achievements:

- **Track Progress:** Regularly review your progress toward your goals. Recognize and celebrate your achievements, no matter how small.

- **Acknowledge Efforts:** Give yourself credit for the effort and determination you put into working toward your goals.

3. Cultivate Self-Compassion:

3.1. Practice Self-Kindness:

- **Be Gentle with Yourself:** Treat yourself with kindness and understanding, especially during difficult times. Avoid self-criticism and practice self-forgiveness.

- **Affirm Your Worth:** Use positive affirmations to reinforce your self-worth. For example, "I am worthy of love and respect" or "I am capable and deserving of success."

3.2. Manage Self-Talk:

- **Monitor Thoughts:** Pay attention to your internal dialogue. Replace self-critical or negative thoughts with affirming and supportive messages.

- **Use Positive Affirmations:** Repeat affirmations that promote self-worth and confidence. Incorporate them into your daily routine to build a more positive self-image.

4. Develop Healthy Relationships:

4.1. Surround Yourself with Supportive People:

- **Build a Support Network:** Cultivate relationships with people who uplift and support you. Seek out friends, family, or mentors who encourage and value you.

- **Set Boundaries:** Establish and maintain boundaries to protect your self-worth and well-being. Avoid relationships or situations that are toxic or undermining.

4.2. Engage in Positive Interactions:

- **Seek Constructive Feedback:** Engage in relationships where you receive constructive and encouraging feedback. Use this feedback to grow and improve.

- **Offer Support:** Support others in their endeavors. Acts of kindness and support can reinforce your sense of self-worth and connection.

5. Focus on Strengths and Achievements:

5.1. Identify Your Strengths:

- **Self-Assessment:** Reflect on your strengths, skills, and talents. Consider past achievements and how they demonstrate your capabilities.

- **Seek Feedback:** Ask others for their perspectives on your strengths and contributions. This can provide additional insights into your value.

5.2. Build on Strengths:

- **Leverage Strengths:** Engage in activities that utilize your strengths and talents. Pursue hobbies, projects, or roles that allow you to excel and feel accomplished.

- **Set Goals Based on Strengths:** Align your goals with your strengths to maximize your potential and satisfaction.

6. Engage in Self-Care and Wellness:

6.1. Prioritize Physical Health:

- **Exercise Regularly:** Engage in physical activities that you enjoy. Exercise can boost your mood and self-esteem.

- **Maintain a Healthy Lifestyle:** Focus on balanced nutrition, adequate sleep, and overall well-being.

6.2. Practice Emotional Well-Being:

- **Mindfulness and Relaxation:** Practice mindfulness, meditation, or relaxation techniques to manage stress and maintain emotional balance.

- **Seek Enjoyment:** Engage in activities that bring you joy and fulfillment. Prioritize self-care routines that nurture your well-being.

7. Pursue Personal Growth and Learning:

7.1. Invest in Learning:

- **Continuing Education:** Pursue opportunities for learning and growth, such as courses, workshops, or new skills. Personal development can enhance your sense of accomplishment and self-worth.

- **Explore New Interests:** Try new activities or hobbies to broaden your experiences and discover new aspects of yourself.

7.2. Embrace Challenges:

- **Face Challenges:** Embrace challenges as opportunities for growth. Tackling difficulties can build resilience and reinforce your sense of self-efficacy.

- **Reflect on Experiences:** Reflect on how overcoming challenges has contributed to your personal growth and self-worth.

8. Seek Professional Support if Needed:

8.1. Consider Therapy:

- **Therapeutic Support:** A therapist can help you explore underlying issues related to self-worth and provide tools and strategies for enhancing it.

- **Cognitive Behavioral Therapy (CBT):** CBT can be particularly effective in addressing negative thought patterns and building self-esteem.

8.2. Join Support Groups:

- **Connect with Others:** Support groups can provide a sense of community and shared experiences. Engaging with others who have similar challenges can offer additional support and perspectives.

Conclusion:

Enhancing self-worth involves recognizing and challenging negative beliefs, setting and achieving goals, cultivating self-compassion, and focusing on your strengths. Building healthy relationships, engaging in self-care, pursuing personal growth, and seeking professional support when needed further contribute to a positive sense of self-worth. By consistently applying these strategies, you can develop a stronger and more positive self-image, leading to a more fulfilling and confident life.

Exercise 8.1: Self-Worth Reflection: Identify strengths and positive qualities about yourself.

Objective: To reflect on your strengths and positive qualities, helping you recognize and affirm your inherent value.

Step 1: Reflect on Your Strengths

Take a moment to think about the qualities, skills, or attributes that you value in yourself. These can be personal strengths (e.g., kindness, perseverance) or skills (e.g., problem-solving, creativity). Write down at least 3-5 strengths that you believe contribute to who you are.

Example Strengths:

"I am a good listener and show empathy to others."
"I am persistent and can keep going even when things get tough."
"I am creative and enjoy finding new solutions to problems."

Your Strengths:

____

____

____

____

____

Step 2: Identify Positive Feedback from Others

Think of at least one instance where someone has complimented you or expressed appreciation for something you've done or who you are. This could be a friend, family member, colleague, or even a stranger. What did they recognize in you? This feedback can serve as external validation of your positive qualities.

Example Feedback:

"My friend always tells me how much they appreciate my ability to stay calm and solve problems in stressful situations."

"My colleague mentioned how much they admire my creative ideas in team meetings."

Your Positive Feedback:

____

____

____

Step 3: Reflect on Your Achievements

Think about some of your past accomplishments that made you proud, whether in your personal life, career, or other areas. These could be big or small, and they help reinforce your sense of self-worth. Write down at least two achievements you are proud of.

Example Achievements:

"I completed a challenging project at work and received praise from my manager."

"I helped a friend through a tough time, and they thanked me for being there for them."

Your Achievements:

____

____

____

Step 4: Acknowledge Your Positive Impact on Others

Think about how your presence, actions, or words have positively impacted those around you. This could be a simple act of kindness or something more significant. Reflect on the ripple effect you create in the lives of others.

Example Reflection:

"I helped my colleague navigate a difficult situation at work, and it made their day easier."

"By volunteering at a local charity, I made a difference in my community."

Your Positive Impact:

____

____

____

Step 5: Write a Self-Worth Affirmation

After reflecting on your strengths, positive feedback, achievements, and impact, write an affirmation that reinforces your self-worth. This could be a statement like, "I am valuable and capable," or "I have many qualities that contribute to my success and happiness." Repeat this affirmation to yourself regularly to build confidence.

Example Affirmation:

"I am worthy of love and respect, and I am proud of the person I am becoming."

Your Self-Worth Affirmation:

____

____

____

Step 6: Reflect and Commit to Self-Acceptance

Take a moment to reflect on the exercise. How do you feel about yourself after identifying your strengths, achievements, and positive qualities? Commit to accepting and appreciating yourself for who you are, even when facing challenges. Remember that your self-worth is inherent and not dependent on external validation.

Reflection:

"I realize I have many positive qualities, and I am proud of what I bring to the world. I am deserving of respect and kindness, starting with myself."

Summary:

This **Self-Worth Reflection** exercise helps you identify the positive qualities, strengths, and achievements that contribute to your value. By focusing on what you bring to the table, you can reinforce a healthy sense of self-worth and cultivate self-acceptance. Regularly practicing this reflection helps build confidence and reminds you of your inherent value, no matter the challenges you face.

Exercise 8.2: Affirmations and Self-Care: Develop a routine for self-affirmation and self-care.

Objective: To create a simple, sustainable routine that incorporates both self-affirmations and self-care practices, promoting a positive mindset and emotional well-being.

Step 1: Identify Your Personal Affirmations

Start by writing down 3-5 positive affirmations that resonate with you. These should be statements that reinforce your worth, strength, and potential. You can create affirmations based on your current goals, challenges, or values. The key is that they should help shift your mindset to one of self-empowerment and positivity.

Example Affirmations:

"I am worthy of love, success, and happiness."
"I am capable of overcoming any challenge that comes my way."
"I trust in my ability to create positive change in my life."

Your Affirmations:

____

____

____

____

____

Step 2: Create a Self-Affirmation Routine

Decide when and how you will incorporate your affirmations into your day. A good time might be in the morning, right after you wake up, or at night before bed. Consider adding affirmations to moments when you need an emotional boost or clarity.

Example Routine:

"I will repeat my affirmations every morning when I wake up while looking in the mirror to connect with myself."

"I will take a few moments before bed to write my affirmations in my journal to reflect on my day and reinforce my self-worth."

Your Affirmation Routine:

- **Time of Day:** _______________________________________
- **Method (speaking, writing, reflecting, etc.):**

  ____
- **Location (e.g., mirror, journal, quiet space):**

  ____

Step 3: Plan Your Daily Self-Care Activities

Self-care can be anything that nurtures your physical, emotional, or mental well-being. It might include relaxation activities, hobbies, exercise, or time for rest. Write down at least 3-5 self-care activities you can easily integrate into your daily life. Focus on small, manageable practices that make you feel cared for and rejuvenated.

Example Self-Care Activities:

"I will take a 10-minute walk every morning to clear my mind."

"I will read for 15 minutes before bed to unwind."

"I will spend time in nature at least once a week to relax and recharge."

Your Self-Care Activities:

———————————————————————————

———————————————————————————

———————————————————————————

———————————————————————————

———————————————————————————

Step 4: Set Realistic Self-Care Goals

Determine which self-care activities you want to commit to and when you will do them. Set realistic and achievable goals for how often you can practice self-care, whether daily, a few times a week, or when you feel you need it most. Consistency is key to making self-care a habit.

Example Goal:

"I will practice my self-care routine every morning before starting my workday, ensuring I take time for myself daily."

Your Self-Care Goals:

1. **Activity 1:** _______________________________________

Frequency: _______________________________________

Goal: _______________________________________

2. **Activity 2:** _______________________________________

Frequency: _______________________________________

Goal: _______________________________________

Step 5: Track Your Progress and Adjust

For the next week, track your progress in following both your self-affirmation routine and self-care activities. Reflect on how you're feeling emotionally, mentally, and physically. Are you experiencing more positivity, calmness, or clarity? Are there areas where you need to adjust your routine to make it more effective or enjoyable?

Reflection Questions:

- "How did I feel after practicing my affirmations each day?"
- "Did I notice any positive shifts in my mindset or energy levels?"
- "Was I able to follow through with my self-care activities? If not, what adjustments can I make?"

Step 6: Celebrate Your Efforts

Acknowledge your commitment to taking care of yourself and reinforcing positive self-beliefs. Celebrate the small victories—whether it's successfully incorporating affirmations into your day or completing a self-care activity. Remember, self-compassion is an essential part of this process.

Example Celebration:

"I will reward myself with a quiet evening of reading and relaxation after a week of practicing affirmations and self-care."

Your Celebration:

____

____

____

Summary:

This **Affirmations and Self-Care Routine** helps you integrate daily practices that nurture your emotional and mental well-being. By committing to a set of affirmations and self-care activities, you are fostering a positive relationship with yourself, reinforcing your self-worth, and making self-care a priority in your life.

Chapter 9

Understanding Maslow's Hierarchy and Personal Growth

Personal growth isn't a straight line; it's a journey of evolution, building on the foundation of who we are and the needs we have at each stage of our lives. The psychologist Abraham Maslow developed a model that helps us understand the process of human development. This roadmap illustrates how we move through different stages of need, from survival to self-actualization. His *Hierarchy of Needs* shows us that before we can achieve our highest potential, we must first meet the fundamental needs that form the foundation of our well-being. These needs are not isolated—they are interconnected, and each one builds upon the last, guiding us toward emotional, psychological, and spiritual growth.

At the base of Maslow's pyramid are the most basic, survival-based needs. As we move upward, we encounter more complex emotional and psychological needs until we reach the peak: self-actualization, the realization of our fullest potential. But why does this hierarchy matter? Because without understanding the stages of our growth—without recognizing where we are in our own journey—we can get stuck in a cycle of unmet needs, perpetuating feelings of inadequacy, isolation, and even worthlessness. And when we don't understand where we are, we also don't understand how to move forward, how to ask for help, or why we feel so stuck.

Imagine, for a moment, the fox caught in the bear trap. The trap is pain, a physical need for survival, and all the fox can think about is escaping. It's in crisis mode, focused entirely on the immediate threat, unable to perceive the larger picture. At this moment, it cannot think about what comes next or what other needs might arise. It is simply surviving. In this way, the fox mirrors the first level of Maslow's Hierarchy—physiological needs—the basic needs for food, water, shelter, and safety. When we are in a crisis or in the grips of pain, our survival instincts take over, and we are often consumed with the immediate struggle for relief. This is the state many of us find ourselves in when we feel helpless, hopeless, and overwhelmed.

Once the basic needs are met, we move upward in the pyramid to safety needs—the need for stability, security, and a sense of protection. Just like the fox in the trap, the immediate pain of the situation must be addressed before it can feel safe enough to trust the hand reaching out. If we feel unsafe in the world—emotionally or physically—we can't begin to address the more complex aspects of life, like relationships, self-esteem, or personal growth. It's only when we feel safe and secure that we can begin to open ourselves up to the possibility of support and connection.

Next, we encounter belonging and love needs—the need to form meaningful relationships, to feel loved and connected. The fox, even once released from the trap, may still struggle with trust. It may fear that no one will ever care for it again or that it's too broken to be embraced. Likewise, many of us, when we feel unworthy or rejected, are hesitant to ask for help because we doubt our place in the world. If we don't believe we belong or are loved, it becomes much harder to lean on others. But when we feel supported and cared for, we are far more likely to reach out, to ask for help, and to open ourselves up to the healing power of connection.

The next level in Maslow's hierarchy is esteem needs—the desire for self-respect, recognition, and the confidence to navigate the world. The fox, now healed, must relearn its own strength. It may feel afraid to move forward, to trust in its own ability to survive and thrive. Similarly, when we feel worthless, it becomes incredibly difficult to ask for help because we don't believe we deserve it. But as we build our self-esteem—by confronting negative beliefs, achieving small successes, and recognizing our inherent worth—we begin to trust ourselves and the people who offer help, support, and encouragement.

Finally, we reach self-actualization—the pinnacle of Maslow's pyramid. This is the realization of our true potential, where we live authentically and embrace our full capacity for creativity, love, and growth. At this stage, asking for help becomes less of an obstacle and more of an opportunity. When we are connected to our authentic selves and understand our place in the world, we are more open to collaboration, to sharing our vulnerabilities, and to receiving help. We no longer see asking for help as a sign of weakness but as a natural part of the process of personal evolution. It's through this vulnerability that we continue to grow, expand, and become who we are truly meant to be.

Maslow's Hierarchy of Needs teaches us that we cannot skip steps in our own growth. Each stage is essential for building the foundation for the next. It also reminds us that personal growth is a process, not a destination. To truly move forward—to ask for help, to heal, and to evolve—we must first understand where we are in our journey, address the needs that are currently unmet, and give ourselves permission to grow at our own pace. Only then can we begin to break free from the traps that hold us back and embrace the support that is available to us.

Objective: Apply Maslow's Hierarchy of Needs to your personal development and the process of seeking help.

Understanding and applying Maslow's Hierarchy of Needs to your life involves recognizing and addressing the various levels of needs described by Abraham Maslow, ultimately working towards self-actualization. Maslow's hierarchy is often depicted as a pyramid with five levels, where each level must be fulfilled before progressing to the next. Here's a breakdown of the hierarchy and how you can apply it to your life:

Maslow's Hierarchy of Needs:

1. **Physiological Needs:** Basic, essential needs for survival.

2. **Safety Needs:** Security and stability in various aspects of life.

3. **Love and Belongingness Needs:** Social relationships, love, and a sense of belonging.

4. **Esteem Needs:** Self-esteem, respect from others, and recognition.

5. **Self-Actualization:** Realizing your full potential and pursuing personal growth.

1. Physiological Needs:

Understanding These Needs:

- **Definition:** Physiological needs include basic requirements for survival, such as food, water, shelter, and sleep.

- **Significance:** These are the most fundamental needs. If they are not met, it's difficult to focus on higher-level needs.

Application:

- **Assess Your Needs:** Ensure that your basic needs are met. Evaluate your diet, living conditions, and overall health.

- **Develop Healthy Habits:** Prioritize activities that support your physical well-being, such as regular exercise, balanced nutrition, and adequate sleep.

2. Safety Needs:

Understanding These Needs:

- **Definition:** Safety needs encompass physical safety, financial stability, health security, and a safe environment.
- **Significance:** Feeling secure is essential for pursuing higher needs. Instability in this area can cause significant stress and hinder personal development.

Application:

- **Financial Security:** Create a budget, build an emergency fund, and seek stable employment or career opportunities.
- **Health and Safety:** Ensure you have access to healthcare and live in a safe environment. Take steps to address any threats to your physical or psychological safety.
- **Plan for the Future:** Set long-term goals and create plans to ensure ongoing stability and security.

3. Love and Belongingness Needs:

Understanding These Needs:

- **Definition:** These needs involve relationships, love, and a sense of belonging within a community or social group.
- **Significance:** Social connections are crucial for emotional well-being and provide support and validation.

Application:

- **Cultivate Relationships:** Invest time and effort in building and maintaining meaningful relationships with family, friends, and romantic partners.

- **Engage in Communities:** Join social groups, clubs, or organizations where you can connect with others who share your interests and values.

- **Improve Communication:** Develop skills to communicate effectively and resolve conflicts to strengthen your relationships.

4. Esteem Needs:

Understanding These Needs:

- **Definition:** Esteem needs include self-esteem, confidence, and recognition from others. This involves feeling valued and respected.

- **Significance:** Meeting these needs contributes to a positive self-image and encourages motivation and achievement.

Application:

- **Set Achievable Goals:** Establish personal and professional goals. Achieving these goals can enhance your self-esteem and provide a sense of accomplishment.

- **Seek Feedback:** Actively seek constructive feedback and recognition from peers, mentors, or supervisors.

- **Build Self-Confidence:** Engage in activities that build your skills and confidence. Practice self-affirmations and challenge negative self-beliefs.

5. Self-Actualization:

Understanding These Needs:

- **Definition:** Self-actualization involves realizing your full potential, pursuing personal growth, creativity, and self-fulfillment. It's about becoming the best version of yourself.
- **Significance:** This is the pinnacle of Maslow's hierarchy and involves continuous personal development and self-improvement.

Application:

- **Identify Your Passions:** Reflect on your interests, values, and goals. Pursue activities and projects that align with your passions and give you a sense of purpose.
- **Embrace Creativity:** Engage in creative pursuits and explore new ways to express yourself. Creativity can enhance your sense of fulfillment and self-discovery.
- **Set Personal Growth Goals:** Focus on continuous learning and self-improvement. Take up new challenges, seek educational opportunities, and work on personal development.
- **Practice Mindfulness and Reflection:** Regularly reflect on your experiences, achievements, and areas for growth. Mindfulness can help you stay connected to your goals and values.

6. Integrate the Hierarchy into Your Life:

6.1. Evaluate Your Needs:

- **Conduct a Self-Assessment:** Regularly assess where you stand in terms of fulfilling each level of needs. Identify any gaps or areas that require attention.

- **Create a Plan:** Develop a plan to address unmet needs, starting from the base of the hierarchy and working upwards. This helps ensure that you're building a strong foundation for self-actualization.

6.2. Balance and Adjust:

- **Maintain Balance:** Ensure that you're addressing all levels of needs, not just focusing on self-actualization. A balanced approach contributes to overall well-being.

- **Adapt and Adjust:** Be flexible and willing to adjust your goals and plans as your needs and circumstances change.

Conclusion:

Applying Maslow's Hierarchy of Needs to your life involves addressing each level of needs, from physiological to self-actualization. By ensuring that your basic needs are met, creating a safe and supportive environment, building meaningful relationships, fostering self-esteem, and pursuing personal growth, you can work towards self-actualization and live a fulfilling and purposeful life. Regular self-assessment and adjustment are key to maintaining balance and achieving ongoing personal development.

Exercise 9.1: Needs Assessment: Map out where you stand on Maslow's hierarchy and identify unmet needs.

Objective: To assess where you stand on Maslow's Hierarchy of Needs and identify any unmet needs that may be affecting your well-being or personal growth.

Step 1: Understand Maslow's Hierarchy of Needs

Maslow's Hierarchy of Needs is a psychological theory that describes human motivation in terms of five levels of needs, from basic to higher-level needs. The levels, from bottom to top, are:

1. **Physiological Needs**: Basic needs like food, water, shelter, and rest.
2. **Safety Needs**: Security, stability, and freedom from fear or threat.
3. **Love and Belonging Needs**: Relationships, social connections, and a sense of community.
4. **Esteem Needs**: Self-respect, self-esteem, recognition, and a sense of accomplishment.
5. **Self-Actualization**: Personal growth, fulfillment of potential, and creativity.

Step 2: Assess Your Current Status in Each Area

For each of the five levels of Maslow's Hierarchy, reflect on your current situation. Are your needs being met in that area? Are there unmet needs that might be holding you back from personal growth or happiness? Rate your current satisfaction in each area on a scale from 1 (very dissatisfied) to 5 (completely satisfied).

Example Assessment:

1. **Physiological Needs** (Food, shelter, rest):

- *How are your basic needs being met?*
- *Do you have enough access to food, water, and sleep?*

   Rating: 4 – "I have my basic needs met, but sometimes I struggle to get enough rest."

2. **Safety Needs** (Security, stability, freedom from fear):

- *Do you feel safe in your living and work environments?*
- *Are there any sources of ongoing anxiety or insecurity?*

   Rating: 3 – "I have a stable job and living situation, but I sometimes worry about financial stability."

3. **Love and Belonging Needs** (Relationships, connections, community):

- *Do you have supportive relationships with family, friends, or a romantic partner?*
- *Do you feel connected to a community or group?*

   Rating: 2 – "I feel a lack of connection with others and would like to nurture deeper relationships."

4. **Esteem Needs** (Self-respect, recognition, achievement):

- *Do you feel respected by others and confident in your own abilities?*
- *Are you recognized for your contributions at work or in your personal life?*

Rating: 3 – "I sometimes doubt my abilities and feel I lack recognition at work."

5. **Self-Actualization Needs** (Growth, potential, creativity):

- *Are you working towards personal goals or pursuing your passions?*
- *Do you feel fulfilled and engaged in activities that challenge and inspire you?*

Rating: 2 – "I am not actively pursuing my dreams and feel a lack of personal growth."

Step 3: Identify Unmet Needs

Review your ratings for each category. Any area rated below a 4 may indicate an unmet need that requires attention. Write down the specific needs you feel are unmet or underdeveloped in your life. Reflect on how these unmet needs may be affecting your overall well-being.

Example Unmet Needs:

- **Safety Needs**: "I often feel anxious about my financial security, even though I have a steady income."

- **Love and Belonging Needs**: "I feel disconnected from friends and family, and I lack a sense of community."

- **Esteem Needs**: "I sometimes struggle with self-doubt, especially at work, and feel like my achievements go unnoticed."

- **Self-Actualization Needs**: "I don't feel like I'm pursuing the things I'm truly passionate about, and I'm not growing as a person."

Your Unmet Needs:

1. **Physiological Needs**:

    ____

2. **Safety Needs**:

    ____

3. **Love and Belonging Needs**:

    ____

4. **Esteem Needs**:

    ____

5. **Self-Actualization Needs**: ____________________________________

    ____

Step 4: Plan Action Steps for Addressing Unmet Needs

For each area with unmet needs, brainstorm specific action steps you can take to begin fulfilling those needs. These should be practical steps that you can start implementing right away, no matter how small.

Example Action Steps:

- **Safety Needs**: "I will start budgeting to reduce financial anxiety and seek advice on financial planning."

- **Love and Belonging Needs**: "I will make an effort to reach out to an old friend and plan regular catch-ups."

- **Esteem Needs**: "I will ask for feedback at work to gain more recognition and clarity on my strengths."

- **Self-Actualization Needs**: "I will set aside time to explore a new hobby or passion project to reignite my sense of personal growth."

Your Action Steps:

1. **Physiological Needs:**

   ____

2. **Safety Needs:**

   ____

3. **Love and Belonging Needs:**

   ____

4. **Esteem Needs:**

   ____

5. **Self-Actualization Needs:**

   ____

Step 5: Reassess and Reflect Regularly

Once you've developed action steps, commit to revisiting this assessment regularly. Consider tracking your progress and reflecting on how meeting these needs enhances your overall happiness and well-being. Reassess your needs every few months to ensure you stay on track with personal growth.

Example Reflection:

"After a month of working on my financial stability and reconnecting with friends, I feel more secure and less anxious. My relationships have deepened, and I feel more recognized at work."

Your Reflection:

____

____

____

Summary:

This **Needs Assessment** helps you identify where you stand on Maslow's Hierarchy and where your needs may be unmet. By recognizing these areas, you can take actionable steps to fulfill your basic needs and move toward self-actualization, improving your overall well-being and personal development.

Exercise 9.2: Growth Plan: Create a plan to address these needs and support your overall growth.

Objective: To create a structured plan for fulfilling unmet needs and promoting growth across different areas of your life, based on the needs identified in the previous exercise.

Step 1: Review the Unmet Needs

Start by reviewing the unmet needs you identified in the **Needs Assessment**. These will guide the focus of your growth plan. Write them down here for clarity.

Your Unmet Needs (from Needs Assessment):

1. **Physiological Needs:**

    ____

2. **Safety Needs:**

    ____

3. **Love and Belonging Needs:**

    ____

4. **Esteem Needs:**

    ____

5. **Self-Actualization Needs:**

    ____

Step 2: Set Clear Growth Goals

For each unmet need, set a clear, actionable goal that addresses the specific area of growth. These goals should be **SMART** (Specific, Measurable, Achievable, Relevant, and Time-bound). Define the desired outcome for each area of your life.

Example Growth Goals:

1. **Physiological Needs:**

Goal: "Ensure that I am getting 7-8 hours of sleep each night for the next month."

Action Steps:

- Set a consistent bedtime.
- Reduce screen time 30 minutes before bed.
- Practice relaxation techniques (e.g., deep breathing or reading) before sleep.

2. **Safety Needs:**

Goal: "Build a basic emergency savings fund of $500 within the next 3 months."

Action Steps:

- Review the current budget and track monthly spending.
- Set aside a fixed amount each week for savings.
- Research and implement simple financial planning strategies.

3. **Love and Belonging Needs:**

Goal: "Reconnect with at least two close friends over the next month."

Action Steps:

- Reach out to a friend via text or call once a week.
- Plan a meetup or virtual hangout.
- Join a community activity (e.g., a hobby group or a fitness class) to meet new people.

4. **Esteem Needs:**

Goal: "Seek constructive feedback from my manager or peers once a month to enhance my self-esteem and career development."

Action Steps:

- Schedule regular check-ins with my manager.
- Reflect on feedback and set goals for improvement.
- Document achievements to recognize personal progress.

5. **Self-Actualization Needs:**

Goal: "Dedicate 30 minutes daily to a personal passion or project for the next month."

Action Steps:

- Block out time in my schedule for personal development.
- Choose a passion or skill I want to develop (e.g., writing, painting, learning a new language).
- Track progress and celebrate small milestones.

Step 3: Create an Action Plan and Timeline

Now that you have clear goals, break down each goal into **specific action steps** and create a **timeline** for implementation. Organize these goals into short-term (1-2 months), medium-term (3-6 months), and long-term (6+ months) milestones.

Example Timeline:

1. **Short-Term Goals (1-2 months):**
   - Improve sleep schedule and consistency.
   - Start saving money for an emergency fund.
   - Reconnect with at least one close friend.
   - Set up a habit of seeking feedback at work.
   - Dedicate time to exploring a personal passion project.

2. **Medium-Term Goals (3-6 months):**
   - Complete building the emergency savings fund.
   - Regularly participate in social or community events.
   - Take on a small challenge related to your self-actualization goal (e.g., finish a small project related to your passion).
   - Cultivate consistent self-affirmation and reflection.

3. **Long-Term Goals (6+ months):**
   - Build long-lasting relationships that provide a sense of belonging.
   - Achieve a sense of recognition or accomplishment in your career.
   - Reach a deeper level of personal growth and fulfillment in your passion or goals.

Step 4: Track Progress and Reflect

To stay on track, set aside time each week or month to track your progress. Reflect on what is working, what needs adjustment, and what you've learned about yourself. You can keep a journal, use an app, or simply make a checklist to track your milestones.

Reflection Questions:

"What progress have I made toward meeting my needs?"

"What changes or adjustments do I need to make in my approach?"

"How do I feel about the progress I've made in my self-care and personal growth?"

Example Reflection:

"I've successfully been reaching out to friends regularly and have noticed an improvement in my emotional well-being. I need to focus more on developing my career goals and seeking more feedback."

Step 5: Adjust and Celebrate Successes

As you implement your growth plan, remember that it's normal to encounter challenges. The key is to adjust your plan as needed while celebrating even small successes along the way. Acknowledge your progress, and reward yourself for each milestone you reach.

Example Adjustments:

- If you're struggling with sleep, try adjusting your bedtime routine further or seeking advice on improving sleep hygiene.

- If you feel disconnected from your social circle, explore new ways to connect with others (e.g., virtual groups, hobby meetups).

Celebration Ideas:

Treat yourself to something meaningful when you hit a goal, such as a relaxing weekend or a small reward that aligns with your interests.

Summary:

This **Growth Plan** helps you address unmet needs across the levels of Maslow's Hierarchy by setting clear, actionable goals, creating an action plan with timelines, and tracking your progress. Regular reflection and celebration will keep you motivated as you work toward greater well-being and personal growth.

Chapter 10

Developing Personality and Identity – Addressing Distorted Thinking and Suicidal Ideations

The journey of developing a strong sense of self is one of the most essential—and often the most challenging—paths we can take in healing. Without a clear understanding of who we are, we are vulnerable to the distortions of our minds, which can tell us lies about our worth, our future, and our very existence. When we don't know who we are or where we belong, it's easy for the whispers of distorted thinking to take over, reinforcing feelings of hopelessness, worthlessness, and the belief that we are better off gone than facing another day of pain.

At the core of distorted thinking is the idea that we are somehow less than—less than others, less than ourselves, or less than the sum of our potential. These thoughts are the breeding ground for suicidal ideations, which often emerge as a way to escape overwhelming emotional pain or confusion. When our minds distort the truth of who we are, we begin to see our lives through a dark lens: one that exaggerates our flaws, minimizes our strengths, and convinces us that there is no way out of our suffering. The belief that we are unworthy of love or happiness can become so consuming that the thought of seeking help, or even continuing on, feels like a distant, unreachable option.

Imagine, again, the fox caught in the bear trap. Its leg is trapped and bloodied, and every instinct tells it that the only way to escape is to gnaw through its own flesh, to hurt itself even more in order to break free. This is often how distorted thinking works—it convinces us that the only way out of pain is through more pain and that the only way to end the suffering is to give in to it completely. The fox, however, is not seeing the larger picture. It cannot see that there is a way out beyond its immediate struggle. It does not yet trust that help is available. And in this moment of crisis, the fox believes that it is alone, that it has no other choice but to suffer in silence.

Similarly, when we are caught in the cycle of distorted thinking, we can become trapped in our own pain. We don't see the possibility of a different reality because we are so consumed by the false narratives in our heads. These thoughts, much like the trap, seem like they are all-encompassing—there is no escape, no other way out. Suicidal ideations are often the culmination of this distorted thinking—a desperate plea for release from pain that feels endless and insurmountable.

But the truth is that distorted thinking is not the truth. These thoughts are based on a false perception of self—one that does not reflect the fullness of who we are or what we are capable of. And just as the fox cannot escape the bear trap alone, we cannot free ourselves from the grip of these thoughts without first developing a sense of self that is strong enough to challenge them.

Developing personality and identity is the key to breaking free from these destructive thought patterns. It is through the process of self-exploration, self-acceptance, and self-compassion that we begin to combat distorted thinking. By getting to know ourselves—our strengths, our values, our passions, and our worth—we can start to see that the negative beliefs we hold about ourselves are not reflections of reality but rather the products of pain, trauma, or misinformation.

When we are clear about who we are and what we stand for, we are better equipped to recognize when our thoughts are skewed or harmful. Our identity becomes a compass, guiding us away from the lies we've been telling ourselves and toward the truth of who we are. This clarity helps us to challenge the distorted thinking that feeds suicidal ideations, allowing us to replace feelings of worthlessness with an understanding of our intrinsic value.

This process doesn't happen overnight—it's a journey, one that takes time and patience. Just like the fox must learn to trust the hunter to release it from the trap, we must learn to trust in our own worth and the possibility of healing. We must learn that we are not defined by our struggles but by our resilience, our capacity to grow, and our potential to thrive. We must learn that asking for help is not a sign of weakness but a step toward reclaiming our power, our identity, and our future.

In this chapter, we will explore how developing a strong sense of self can serve as a powerful antidote to distorted thinking and suicidal ideations. We'll dive into the importance of understanding who we are, what makes us unique, and how we can use this understanding to challenge the negative thoughts that cloud our vision and keep us trapped in emotional darkness. By building a clearer, more grounded sense of self, we can begin to see that our lives have immense value— and that no matter how intense the storm of thoughts may be, there is always hope, always help, and always a way forward.

Objective: Explore your personality and identity while tackling distorted thinking and addressing suicidal ideations.

Developing Personality and Identity

Developing personality and identity is a dynamic and ongoing process influenced by various factors, including experiences, relationships, and personal growth. Here's a structured approach to help you develop a stronger sense of self:

1. Understanding Personality and Identity:

1.1. Personality:

- **Definition:** Personality encompasses your unique patterns of thinking, feeling, and behaving. It includes traits and characteristics that define how you interact with the world.

- **Development:** Personality is shaped by genetics, upbringing, life experiences, and personal choices. It evolves over time as you gain new experiences and insights.

1.2. Identity:

- **Definition:** Identity refers to your sense of self and how you perceive your role and place in the world. It includes aspects like values, beliefs, roles, and self-concept.

- **Development:** Identity develops through self-exploration, reflection, and feedback from others. It's influenced by your experiences, relationships, and personal growth.

2. Explore and Reflect:

2.1. Self-Exploration:

- **Identify Interests and Passions:** Explore activities, hobbies, and interests that resonate with you. Reflect on what you enjoy and what gives you a sense of purpose.

- **Assess Values and Beliefs:** Consider your core values and beliefs. What principles guide your decisions and actions? Understanding your values can help you align your life with what matters most to you.

2.2. Reflect on Experiences:

- **Journaling:** Keep a journal to document your thoughts, feelings, and experiences. Reflect on how these experiences shape your personality and identity.

- **Seek Feedback:** Talk to trusted friends, family members, or mentors about your personality and identity. Their perspectives can provide valuable insights.

3. Set Goals and Pursue Growth:

3.1. Personal Goals:

- **Define Your Goals:** Set goals that align with your interests, values, and aspirations. Goals can help you develop and refine aspects of your personality and identity.
- **Create a Plan:** Develop a plan to achieve your goals. Break them into manageable steps and track your progress.

3.2. Engage in Growth Activities:

- **Learn and Explore:** Take up new learning opportunities, such as courses or workshops, to expand your knowledge and skills. Explore new environments and experiences to gain broader perspectives.
- **Challenge Yourself:** Step out of your comfort zone by taking on new challenges. Personal growth often involves confronting fears and pushing your boundaries.

4. Build and Maintain Relationships:

4.1. Connect with Others:

- **Build Supportive Relationships:** Surround yourself with people who support and encourage your growth. Positive relationships can help you explore and affirm your identity.

- **Engage in Meaningful Interactions:** Participate in activities and groups that foster meaningful connections and allow you to express and develop your personality.

4.2. Reflect on Relationships:

- **Evaluate Relationships:** Reflect on how your relationships influence your sense of self. Consider whether your interactions align with your values and contribute positively to your identity.

- **Seek Feedback:** Use feedback from trusted individuals to gain insights into how others perceive your personality and identity.

5. Practice Self-Awareness and Self-Compassion:

5.1. Self-Awareness:

- **Mindfulness:** Practice mindfulness to increase self-awareness and understanding of your thoughts, feelings, and behaviors.

- **Self-Reflection:** Regularly reflect on your experiences and personal growth. Consider how your actions and choices align with your evolving identity.

5.2. Self-Compassion:

- **Be Kind to Yourself:** Practice self-compassion by treating yourself with kindness and understanding. Acknowledge that personal growth is a continuous process.

- **Accept Imperfection:** Recognize that developing personality and identity involves growth and change. Embrace imperfections as part of your journey.

Challenging Suicidal Ideation Without Knowing Yourself:

When dealing with suicidal ideation, it's essential to address immediate safety and seek support, even if you feel disconnected from your sense of self. Here's how you can approach it:

1. Immediate Safety:

1.1. Seek Professional Help:

- **Reach Out:** Contact a mental health professional, counselor, or therapist. They can provide immediate support and strategies to manage suicidal thoughts.

- **Crisis Resources:** Use crisis resources such as hotlines or emergency services if you're in immediate danger or need urgent support.

1.2. Create a Safety Plan:

- **Identify Triggers:** Work with a therapist to identify triggers for suicidal thoughts and develop strategies to manage them.

- **Emergency Contacts:** List trusted individuals who can provide support in times of crisis. Keep their contact information readily available.

2. Develop Self-Awareness:

2.1. Explore Your Feelings:

- **Journaling:** Begin journaling to explore your thoughts and feelings. Even if you're unsure of your identity, writing can help you process emotions and identify patterns.

- **Reflect on Experiences:** Reflect on experiences that have contributed to your current state. Understanding your emotional triggers can provide insights into your struggles.

2.2. Engage in Self-Care:

- **Prioritize Well-Being:** Engage in self-care activities that support your mental and physical health. This includes maintaining a healthy lifestyle, practicing relaxation techniques, and engaging in activities that bring you joy.

- **Seek Support:** Connect with support groups or community resources that can provide understanding and shared experiences.

3. Work on Identity Exploration:

3.1. Explore Interests and Values:

- **Identify Interests:** Even if you're struggling, exploring interests and hobbies can provide a sense of purpose and direction.

- **Reflect on Values:** Consider what values are important to you, even if they're not fully developed. This can guide your actions and decisions.

3.2. Set Small Goals:

- **Start Small:** Set small, achievable goals that can provide a sense of accomplishment and build confidence.

- **Celebrate Progress:** Recognize and celebrate your achievements, no matter how minor they may seem. Each step forward is valuable.

4. Build Supportive Relationships:

4.1. Connect with Others:

- **Reach Out:** Build connections with supportive individuals who can offer understanding and encouragement.
- **Seek Social Support:** Engage in activities or groups that provide a sense of belonging and connection.

4.2. Reflect on Relationships:

- **Evaluate Support:** Reflect on how your relationships impact your mental health. Seek out relationships that contribute positively to your well-being.
- **Communicate Openly:** Share your feelings and struggles with trusted individuals who can offer support and perspective.

Conclusion:

Developing personality and identity is a continuous process of self-exploration, growth, and reflection. By exploring your interests, values, and relationships, you can build a stronger sense of self. When facing suicidal ideation, prioritize immediate safety, seek professional support, and work on self-awareness and self-care. Addressing immediate challenges and long-term self-development can contribute to a more fulfilling and balanced life.

Exercise 10.1: Personality Exploration: Reflect on your personality traits and how they impact your interactions with others.

Objective: To explore and reflect on your personality traits, how they shape your behavior, and how they impact your relationships with others. This exercise will help increase self-awareness and improve communication and interaction with those around you.

Step 1: Identify Key Personality Traits

Take a few moments to reflect on your core personality traits. These qualities define how you typically behave, think, and interact with others. Write down 3-5 traits that you feel best describe you. Consider both positive and negative traits, as they all contribute to your overall personality.

Example Traits:

- Empathetic
- Introverted
- Assertive
- Perfectionistic
- Open-minded

Your Personality Traits:

____

____

Step 2: Reflect on How These Traits Affect Your Interactions

Now, reflect on how each of these traits impacts your interactions with others. Think about how your personality may influence your communication style, behavior, and relationships. Do your traits help you connect with others or create challenges? Write a brief reflection on each trait.

Example Reflection:

- **Empathetic**: "Being empathetic helps me connect deeply with others and offer support, but it can also lead to emotional exhaustion if I take on others' feelings too much."

- **Introverted**: "My introversion means I often need time alone to recharge, which can sometimes make me seem distant in social situations, but I feel more authentic and energized when I connect with others."

Your Reflections:

1. **Trait:** _______________________________________

   Reflection:

   ____

2. **Trait:** _______________________________________

   Reflection:

   ____

3. **Trait:** _______________________________________

   Reflection:

   ____

4. **Trait:** _______________________________________

   Reflection:

   ____

5. **Trait:** _______________________________________

   Reflection:

   ____

Step 3: Identify Strengths and Challenges

Now that you've reflected on how your personality traits affect your interactions, identify the strengths and challenges that arise from these traits. How do your strengths help you in relationships? What are the challenges that may require more awareness or adjustment?

Example Strengths and Challenges:

- **Strength:** "My empathy allows me to be a good listener and support others in difficult times."

- **Challenge:** "My introversion sometimes makes it hard for me to initiate social interactions, leading to missed opportunities for connection."

Your Strengths and Challenges:

Strength(s):

____

____

____

Challenge(s):

____

____

____

Step 4: Consider How to Leverage Strengths and Address Challenges

Think about ways to make the most of your strengths and address the challenges related to your personality. Are there strategies or changes in behavior you can try to improve your interactions with others? Write down 1-2 strategies for each trait.

Example Strategies:

- **Empathetic**: "I will set boundaries to ensure I don't take on others' emotions too heavily while still offering my support."
- **Introverted**: "I will challenge myself to initiate social interactions more often, even if it's uncomfortable at first, to build stronger connections."

Your Strategies:

1. **Trait:** ____

   Strategies:

   ____

2. **Trait:** ____

   Strategies:

   ____

3. **Trait:** ____

   Strategies:

   ____

4. **Trait:** ____

   Strategies:

   ____

5. **Trait:** ____

Strategies:

Step 5: Reflect on Your Personal Growth

To conclude, reflect on how understanding your personality traits and their impact on your interactions can help you grow personally and in your relationships. Are there any insights you've gained about yourself? How can this knowledge guide your future behavior and interactions with others?

Reflection:

"By understanding that my introversion affects how I engage socially, I can actively work on pushing myself to be more present in social settings. Similarly, recognizing my empathy helps me be more mindful of boundaries, so I don't overwhelm myself."

Summary:

This **Personality Exploration** exercise helps you reflect on your core personality traits and how they shape your relationships with others. By identifying your strengths and challenges, you can work on leveraging your positive traits while addressing areas that may need more awareness or adjustment. Regular reflection on your personality can lead to personal growth, improved communication, and more meaningful interactions with others.

Exercise 10.2: Distorted Thinking Challenge: Identify and reframe distorted thoughts.

Objective: To help you identify common cognitive distortions in your thinking, challenge their validity, and reframe them with healthier, more balanced perspectives. This exercise will help improve emotional resilience and create a more positive mindset.

Step 1: Identify Distorted Thoughts

Start by reflecting on recent situations where you felt upset, anxious, or frustrated. Write down any negative or unhelpful thoughts that you had during those moments. These are often the distorted thoughts that influence how you feel and behave. Some common cognitive distortions include:

- **All-or-Nothing Thinking**: Seeing things as black-and-white, without a middle ground.

- **Overgeneralization**: Making broad conclusions based on a single event.

- **Catastrophizing**: Expecting the worst possible outcome.

- **Personalization**: Taking responsibility for things outside your control.

- **Mind Reading**: Assuming you know what others are thinking.

- **Emotional Reasoning**: Believing that because you feel something, it must be true.

Example:

- **Situation:** A meeting at work didn't go as planned.
- **Distorted Thought:** "I completely messed up, and now my boss will think I'm incompetent."
- **Cognitive Distortion**: All-or-Nothing Thinking / Catastrophizing.

Your Situation & Distorted Thought(s):

1. **Situation**:

   ____

   Distorted Thought:

   ____

2. **Situation**:

   ____

   Distorted Thought:

   ____

Step 2: Challenge the Distorted Thought

Next, challenge the distorted thoughts by asking yourself a series of questions. This will help you evaluate the validity of your thought and identify whether it is based on facts or assumptions.

Questions to ask yourself:

- Is this thought based on facts, or is it an assumption?

- What evidence do I have to support this thought?
- What evidence contradicts this thought?
- Am I jumping to conclusions?
- What would I say to a friend who had this thought?
- Is there a more balanced or realistic way to view the situation?

Example Challenge:

- Distorted Thought: "I completely messed up, and now my boss will think I'm incompetent."
- Evidence For: "I didn't present all my points clearly."
- Evidence Against: "I received positive feedback on my previous projects. One bad meeting doesn't define my abilities."
- More Balanced Thought: "I made a mistake, but I can learn from it and do better next time. It doesn't define my abilities or my worth."

Your Thought Challenge:

1. **Distorted Thought:**

____

Evidence For:

____

Evidence Against:

____

Balanced Thought:

____

2. **Distorted Thought:**

____

Evidence For:

____

Evidence Against:

____

Balanced Thought:

____

Step 3: Reframe Your Thought

Once you've challenged the distorted thought, reframe it with a more balanced and realistic perspective. This reframed thought should help you feel calmer, more empowered, and less overwhelmed.

Example Reframed Thought:

"Although I didn't do as well as I'd hoped in this meeting, it's just one instance. I'll learn from it and continue improving. My boss knows I'm capable."

Your Reframed Thoughts:

1. **Distorted Thought:**

____

Reframed Thought:

____

2. **Distorted Thought:**

____

Reframed Thought:

____

Step 4: Observe the Emotional Shift

Now that you have reframed your thoughts, take a moment to notice how the new, balanced perspective makes you feel. Is your mood or stress level lower? Do you feel more confident or calm? This can help you see how changing your thoughts can positively impact your emotional state.

Reflection:

"After reframing my thoughts about the meeting, I feel less anxious and more focused on how to improve next time. I no longer feel overwhelmed by the mistake."

Your Emotional Shift:

- How do you feel after reframing your thoughts?

____

- What impact did reframing have on your emotions?

____

Step 5: Practice Regularly

Cognitive distortions are automatic and can be hard to recognize at the moment. Make it a habit to practice this exercise regularly, especially when you're feeling stressed or upset. The more you practice identifying and reframing distorted thoughts, the easier it becomes to change your thinking patterns over time.

Reflection:

"I plan to take a few moments each day to check in with my thoughts, challenge any distortions, and reframe them. I'll start using the balanced thought strategy in real-time situations."

Summary:

This **Distorted Thinking Challenge** helps you identify and reframe negative thought patterns, enabling you to shift from a distorted view to a more balanced, realistic perspective. Regularly practicing this exercise will increase your emotional resilience, improve your problem-solving abilities, and help you feel more in control of your thoughts and emotions.

Resource 10.1

Suicidal Ideation Resources: Find and utilize resources for support and intervention if needed.

1. Recognize the Situation and Need for Help:

1.1. Identify the Trap:

- **Awareness:** Understand that you are in a difficult or harmful situation. Recognize the signs of distress or when you're feeling overwhelmed by the problem.

- **Acknowledge Limits:** Accept that you might not have all the solutions or resources needed to handle the situation on your own.

2. Reach Out for Support:

2.1. Identify Support Networks:

- **Seek Trusted Individuals:** Reach out to friends, family, or mentors who can offer advice, support, or assistance. They might provide practical solutions or emotional comfort.

- **Professional Help:** Consider consulting with professionals such as counselors, therapists, or advisors who are trained to handle specific problems or crises.

2.2. Communicate Clearly:

- **Express Needs:** Clearly articulate what you're going through and what kind of help you need. Being specific can make it easier for others to provide the appropriate support.

- **Be Honest:** Share your feelings and challenges openly. Honesty can foster deeper understanding and more effective assistance from others.

3. Utilize Available Resources:

3.1. Explore Options:

- **Research Solutions:** Look into various resources or services that could address your problem. This might include community services, online resources, or support groups.

- **Leverage Tools:** Use tools and resources designed to help individuals in similar situations. For instance, crisis hotlines, mental health apps, or self-help guides can offer immediate support.

3.2. Ask for Guidance:

- **Seek Advice:** Ask for guidance from those who have experienced similar situations or have expertise in the area. Their insights can provide valuable perspectives and solutions.

- **Follow Recommendations:** Act on the advice and suggestions provided by others, and be open to different approaches or strategies.

4. Develop Coping Strategies:

4.1. Create a Plan:

- **Action Steps:** Develop a step-by-step plan to address the immediate problem. Break down the solution into manageable tasks.

- **Safety Measures:** Incorporate safety measures to protect yourself while working through the problem. Ensure you're not putting yourself at further risk.

4.2. Practice Self-Care:

- **Stress Management:** Engage in activities that reduce stress and support mental health, such as exercise, meditation, or hobbies.

- **Healthy Habits:** Maintain a balanced diet, adequate sleep, and other healthy habits to support overall well-being.

5. Learn and Reflect:

5.1. Reflect on the Experience:

- **Evaluate:** After addressing the immediate issue, reflect on what worked, what didn't, and what you learned from the experience.

- **Adjust:** Use these insights to adjust your approach to future challenges and develop more effective coping strategies.

5.2. Build Resilience:

- **Develop Skills:** Focus on building skills and resilience to better handle future difficulties. This might include problem-solving skills, emotional regulation, or seeking help sooner.

Conclusion:

Instead of taking extreme measures like the fox chewing its own leg off, approaching the problem with a clear strategy of recognizing the issue, reaching out for support, utilizing resources, developing coping strategies, and learning from the experience can lead to more constructive and less harmful outcomes. Seeking help is a strength, not a weakness, and it can provide you with the tools and support needed to navigate through difficult situations effectively.

Additional Resources:

- Contact Information for Crisis Support and Counseling Services
- Recommended Books and Articles on Mental Health and Personal Development
- Links to Online Support Communities and Forums

The Power of Asking for Help – My Journey to Healing to truly help others

When I reflect on the years I spent trapped in anxiety, depression, PTSD, substance abuse, chronic pain from cancer, and the stagnation that kept me locked in place, I often think of a fox caught in a bear trap. The pain was immediate and overwhelming, and every instinct told me to escape by pulling harder, by gnawing at the trap that held me, even though that only deepened the wound. I was isolated, struggling alone, convinced that the only way out was through my own strength. Like the fox, I couldn't see any possibility beyond the immediate pain and fear. I couldn't trust that there might be a way out, a way to heal without further self-destruction. My mind was clouded with distorted thinking, telling me I was trapped forever, that I was unworthy of help, and that relief was beyond my reach.

But the truth is, I was never truly alone in that struggle. The key to my healing came when I learned that the trap, the pain, and the belief that I had to handle it all by myself were the true sources of my suffering. Just like the fox needed someone to release it from the trap, I, too, needed to ask for help—to stop pulling at the trap and allow others to help me free myself. I couldn't heal by force alone. I had to learn how to let go of the illusion that I was the only one who could save myself.

In this book, I've shared the tools that I developed from my own healing journey and ones created while working with others that helped me understand my own trap: how identifying the layers of my pain and distorted thinking allowed me to start seeing the path to freedom. But none of these tools alone could have pulled me out of my darkest moments. The pivotal moment in my journey was when I finally recognized that asking for help was not a sign of weakness—it was the act of trusting in my worth and in others. I had to acknowledge that I didn't have to fight this battle on my own.

Sending that email to the officers and ultimately asking for help became my turning point to truly begin my journey of healing and helping. Whether it was reaching out to a therapist for PTSD, opening up to loved ones about my depression, or seeking support to break free from addiction, each call for help was like someone coming to release the trap around my leg. At first, it was hard to trust that others would be there for me—that they wouldn't see me as weak or broken. But over time, I realized that no one can heal alone. Even the most resilient fox can't escape a bear trap without assistance. And I couldn't escape my pain and struggles without leaning on others for support.

Each time I asked for help, I began to see myself differently—not as the fox caught in the trap, but as a being worthy of compassion, care, and healing. With every act of vulnerability, I reclaimed a piece of my identity, a piece of my worth. The distorted thinking that had convinced me I wasn't worthy of love or support began to lose its power. I learned to see my life not through the lens of worthlessness but through the lens of possibility. And the more I asked for help, the more I grew—learning to trust in myself, in others, and in the healing process.

Today, I can stand here and say that I am no longer the fox in the bear trap. I have learned to live with chronic pain, manage my anxiety, and navigate my depression. I have found new ways to address my trauma, not as something that defines me, but as something that has shaped me, something I can heal from. Most importantly, I have learned that asking for help is not a burden—it's a gift. It's a way to acknowledge that I am not alone in this journey and that I deserve the support of others to help me heal.

As you read these words, I want you to know that you, too, are worthy of help. No matter how deep the trap may seem, no matter how heavy the pain, you don't have to struggle alone. Just as the fox couldn't escape the trap without someone else's intervention, you don't have to carry the weight of your struggles alone. Healing is not a solitary endeavor—it's a shared experience. You are not defined by your pain, your trauma, or your struggles. You are defined by your ability to ask for help, to trust in your own worth, and to open yourself to the healing that comes from connection.

So, if you find yourself caught in a trap—whether it's anxiety, depression, PTSD, addiction, or any other form of suffering—remember this: You don't have to fight alone. Asking for help is the first step in freeing yourself from the trap, and it's the key to living a life of connection, growth, and healing.

You deserve to be freed from the trap. And you deserve to ask for help.

www.ingramcontent.com/pod-product-compliance
Lightning Source LLC
Chambersburg PA
CBHW061529120726

48001CB00004B/1451